T0155007

# H. L. Hix

# AMERICAN ANGER

## An Evidentiary

Also by H. L. Hix

POETRY
*I'm Here to Learn to Dream in Your Language* *
*As Much As, If Not More Than* *
*First Fire, Then Birds* *
*Incident Light* *
*Legible Heavens* *
*God Bless* *
*Chromatic* *
*Shadows of Houses* *
*Surely As Birds Fly*
*Rational Numbers*
*Perfect Hell*

TRANSLATIONS
Juhan Liiv, *Snow Drifts, I Sing: Selected Poems*, trans. with Jüri Talvet
Eugenijus Ališanka, *from unwritten histories*, trans. with the author
Jüri Talvet, *Of Snow, of Soul: New Selected Poems*, trans. with the author
Jüri Talvet, *Estonian Elegy: Selected Poems*, trans. with the author
Juhan Liiv, *The Mind Would Bear No Better*, trans. with Jüri Talvet
*On the Way Home: An Anthology of Contemporary Estonian Poetry*,
trans. with Jüri Talvet
Jüri Talvet, *A Call for Cultural Symbiosis*, trans. with the author
Eugenijus Ališanka, *City of Ash*, trans. with the author

ANTHOLOGIES
*Ley Lines*
*Made Priceless: A Few Things Money Can't Buy*
*New Voices: Contemporary Poetry from the United States*
*Wild and Whirling Words: A Poetic Conversation* *

PHILOSOPHY, THEORY, CRITICISM
*Lines of Inquiry* *
*As Easy As Lying: Essays on Poetry* *
*Understanding William H. Gass*
*Understanding W. S. Merwin*
*Spirits Hovering Over the Ashes: Legacies of Postmodern Theory*
*Morte d'Author: An Autopsy*

* Also published by Etruscan Press

# AMERICAN ANGER

## An Evidentiary

### H. L. Hix

etruscan press

© 2015 by H. L. Hix, and Published 2016 by Etruscan Press

All rights reserved. Except for brief quotations in critical articles or reviews, no part of this book may be reproduced in any manner without prior written permission from the publisher:

Etruscan Press
Wilkes University
84 West South Street
Wilkes-Barre, PA 18766
(570) 408-4546

WILKES UNIVERSITY

www.etruscanpress.org

Published 2016 by Etruscan Press
Printed in the United States of America
Cover design, interior design and typesetting by Laurie Powers
The text of this book is set in Adobe Garamond.

The statement on the back cover is reprinted by permission of W. S. Merwin. It is from "An Interview with W. S. Merwin," by Christian McEwen, *The Writer's Chronicle* 47:4 (Feb. 2015): 19.

*First Edition*

16 17 18 19 20 5 4 3 2 1

Library of Congress Cataloguing-in-Publication Data
Hix, H. L.
 [Poems. Selections]
 American anger : an evidentiary / H. L. Hix.
  pages ; cm
 ISBN 978-0-9897532-4-1 (softcover : acid-free paper)
 I. Title.
 PS3558.I88A6 2016
 811'.54--dc23

2015010953
Please turn to the back of this book for a list of the sustaining funders of Etruscan Press.

This book is printed on recycled, acid-free paper.

The history of anger is the history of humankind.

# AGGRESSION CUES

Aggression cues, such as the presence of a gun, can also elicit aggressive behavior in angry people.

**Aggression Cue 1: The presence of a gun.**

This one here is my just-in-case gun.
This one is my what-the-hell gun.
This one is my don't-take-no-shit-from-nobody gun.
That one there is my get-out-of-my-way gun.
    Ø
Angry is as angry does. A rolling ire gathers no moss.
A gun in the hand is worth two in the Walmart. A fool
and his gun are soon parted. Anger makes the heart grow fonder.
    Ø
That's *not* what I said.
    Ø
"Does carrying a firearm outside your home make you feel safer from crime,
or does it make you feel less safe, or doesn't it have much effect
on how safe you feel?" Of gun owners, percentages.
"Does having a gun in your house make you feel more safe from crime,
less safe, or doesn't it make any difference?" Of gun owners, percentages.
    Ø
I can stop the guy breaking in through the window,
but not the one breaking in through the door.
    Ø
A *dispositional* definition of revenge only muddies things.
"I'll make him pay" need match no *motive* or *feeling*.
Does it matter how, in making me pay, you feel?
How, when you take revenge, would I know why you act?
Better a *functional* definition. Not why do you want him to pay,
not are you happy that he had to, but: *Did he pay?*
That counts as revenge all retaliatory impositions of costs,
even those not based on deliberation or awareness,
and those that do not succeed in deterrence
(as when one driver, perceiving aggression
from another, behaves aggressively in return).

**Aggression Cue 2: A hand slammed on a table.**

Courtesy, line one.
PEOPLE NOT SERVICED MUST REMAIN IN LOBBY
Waitchor turn, bitch.
    Ø
Behind every great man there's a fury.  Better chafed than sorry.
Better the pistol you know than the pistol you don't.
Better hate than anger.
    Ø
That's *not* what I said, and you know it.
    Ø
I can stop the flooding, but not the hurricane.
    Ø
Let's distinguish *expressive* from *instrumental*.
Say we're out drinking, and a faggot shows up, or a Jew.
A lesson for him, some fun for us, *that*'s expressive, no?
And different from chasing off the wetbacks that swarm here
like locusts.  I've got a family to feed, a schoolyard
to defend against the drugs and gangs they bring with them.
Expressive, instrumental: which is anger, which is not?  You tell me.
    Ø
My anger welcomes night with spectacular colors
because of the haze between me and it: dust, ash, pollen.
    Ø
One anger visible, one mouse in the kitchen: dozens more in the walls.
    Ø
That's an angry woman in her housecoat shouting
at her neighbor not to shovel his drive so damned early.
That's an angry child cussing out his first-grade teacher.
Those are some words even his teacher didn't know.
That's an angry stretch of strip malls.
That's one angry parking lot.

**Aggression Cue 3: A fist punched through sheetrock.**

Anger is stimulus bound. Our patient with an array
of twenty electrodes implanted in both temporal lobes
displayed no aggression in the laboratory setting,
but the same stimulation to her hippocampus
applied by radio control when she was "chatting
amiably with her psychiatrist" in his office
occasioned rage, incoherence, loss of contact,
a furious, directed attack against the wall.
   Ø
Cheaters never fluster. Children should be mean, and not nerds.
Cut your coat to suit your wrath.
   Ø
That's *not* what I meant.
   Ø
I can stop the raccoon from getting at the chickens,
but not the mice from getting at their corn.
   Ø
Tree in the forest, who knows, but this I can tell you:
people don't stop at stop signs when no one is watching.
   Ø
(As when one employee, perceiving aggression
from another, behaves aggressively in return.)
   Ø
That's an angry neighbor spitting about smoke from a barbecue grill.
*You'll see! THAT house burns COAL all winter.*
That's an angry used-car dealership.
Those are some angry 18-year-old boys with their books closed:
that woman at the front of the classroom looks wildly alone.
Those are some angry seats them boys is slouched in,
bolted into some angry, angry rows.

**Aggression Cue 4: Arms crossed.**

Don't put your elbows on the table.  Chew with your mouth closed.
Watch your cholesterol.  Exercise four days a week.
Mow your lawn.  Eat your peas and be happy.
Cut down on your coffee.  Cut out all that liquor, my god.
Root for the home team.  Don't put weeds in the compost.
Or eggs, or meat, or too much grass.  Don't sass your elders.
Take off your hat when you come inside.  Clean the gutters.
Don't put all your eggs in one basket.  Wash your hands before dinner.
    Ø
Don't put all your rage in one basket.  Do as I say,
or watch what I do.  Devil take the kindest.
    Ø
That's *not* the point.
    Ø
I can stop the rain leaking through the roof,
but not the groundwater seeping into the basement.
    Ø
*Bridge of the Sufferers.  Monument to the Defeated.*
*Meditating Pool in Honor of the Accidentally Drowned.*
*Altar of the Shat Straight from Satan's Chafed Ass.*
Stop with the roadside crosses and plastic flowers, already.
I lost a teenage daughter, too.
*Garden of the Retards.  Testament to the Shiftless.*
*Museum of Didn't Have Much to Start With, Or Get Much Along the Way.*
*Tomb of the Unknown Collateral Damage of Operation Something or Other.*
    Ø
I've got a family to feed, a neighborhood to defend.
    Ø
My anger *keeps* the bourbon bottles and beer cans
assholes toss into the yard when they drive by at night.
Has a heap of them now, out by the shed.

**Aggression Cue 5: Fists clenched.**

Friend of mine a little while in junior high, Jay something.
Middle of the year he moved away, I don't remember where,
don't remember his last name. Junior high was a long time ago,
how much do you expect me to remember? Most of it
seemed forgettable, even then. I remember this, though:
once, just once, he said out loud the thing the rest of us
wouldn't say. *My dad beats me*, he said, *I guess I'll beat my kids.*
By now he's got a grandkid somewhere with a cracked rib
and a split lip thrilling his friends with the same boast.
     Ø
Every little fit helps. Every puncture tells a story.
Empty clips made the most noise.
     Ø
That's *not* the deal we made.
     Ø
That's an angry man driving that custom GTO
that rumbles and squirms when it idles at that light.
That's an angry man picking a fight in this shitty bar.
Those are some angry crows.
     Ø
If I come to an understanding with the spill,
will it hold, too, for the break, and for the infestation?
     Ø
At a physiological level we cannot clearly differentiate fear from anger.
We find no evidence that spontaneous stimuli for fighting arise
within the body of any normal organism. Reactivity to stimuli
varies widely across individuals, but in no case can inner characteristics
*alone* explain aggression. Always environment holds the causative key.
     Ø
(As when one patron, perceiving aggression
from another, behaves aggressively in return.)

**Aggression Cue 6: A uniform.**

Police bias has little to do with how officers act when persons fall
under *incidental* suspicion — when *clues* select the persons to suspect.
Bias appears in *methodical* suspicion, in how and where and at whom
officers look when *no one* falls under incidental suspicion,
when we want suspects but the clues point none out.

     Ø

Failing to arm is aiming to fail.  Finders keepers,
losers shut the fuck up.  First aggressions last longest.
Fortune favors the well-armed.  Flattery
will get you nowhere a gun won't get you faster.

     Ø

That's *not* what you said before.

     Ø

If I come to an understanding with the surgery,
will it hold, too, for the regimen of poisons imposed after?

     Ø

I've got a family to feed, a principle to defend.

     Ø

Count 'em.  In Watts, of the thirty-four killed, thirty-one were black.
At least twenty-eight were shot by police and National Guard.
The victims included two men shot as supposed snipers,
each while standing unarmed at a window of his own home,
neither with a weapon on the premises but each wearing a white t-shirt
that made him visible inside.  One man shot while removing
household effects from his own home, which was threatened
by a fire nearby.  One shot while standing on his own front lawn.
In each instance, the coroner's jury reached a verdict,
after briefest inquest, of justifiable homicide.

     Ø

My anger only *looks* clear, held in a glass.
In fact, Fever swims in it, and Contagion.

**Aggression Cue 7: The gathering of a crowd.**

Q: Why have you and your neighbors assembled for military drill?
A: Such tyrannical efforts was the government using that there would be
a time come when we should have to stand in defense of our rights.
Q: Did you feel the tyranny of the government yourself?
A: We were afraid the government would crowd us.
Q: Did the government crowd you any?
A: No, but there had been talk.

    Ø

Genius is one percent inspiration, ninety-nine percent superior weaponry.
God helps those who arm themselves.  Good shotguns make good neighbors.
Good things come to those who don't take no shit.

    Ø

That's *not* what they said when I called your office.

    Ø

That's an angry man whipping his son a little harder
than he needs to, and a lot more often.
That's an angry woman yelling for her daughter at the t-ball game.
Those are some angry clouds.  That's one angry squirrel.

    Ø

If I come to an understanding with the blight,
will it hold, too, for the detonation, and for the drought?

    Ø

We sons of God sow violence upon the earth.  In Scripture,
each time a man of God rose up, the forces of evil
rose against him.  In history, the two periods with the most
demonic activity were when Jesus was walking the earth,
and now.  The more we do what God wants, the more we walk
in the power and spirit of God, the more violence will increase.

    Ø

(As when one passenger, perceiving aggression
from another, behaves aggressively in return.)

**Aggression Cue 8: The presence of an aircraft carrier.**

Soon enough, war is life, and life war.  Every act of violence,
every act of government gets construed as an act of war.
Every protester, every stone-throwing child becomes
an enemy combatant: imprisoned without trial, tortured,
"disappeared."  Public life follows a military logic,
with all that does not hasten victory pushed aside.
  Ø
If a right is worth defending, it is worth defending well.
If at first you don't succeed, try a semi-automatic.
If it ain't broke, damned if I'm gonna let *you* break it.
If you can't beat 'em, you need more target practice.
It ain't over till somebody finally pops the damn fat lady.
  Ø
That's *not* what I want to hear right now.
  Ø
For a while you reason or plead, but then you lash out.
  Ø
Sure, go stop the genocides in Bosnia, Somalia, Timbuktu, what the fuck.
But if they can't disarm the gangs and drug dealers here in St. Louis,
how do they plan to somewhere else?  Let 'em take down the Taliban,
cut off the warlords, but *after* they secure my sidewalk, for chrissake,
so I can make it safely from my house to my car.
  Ø
I've got my family to feed, my honor to defend.
  Ø
Thank God for the Holocaust, and for Rwanda,
others' shimmering genocides, not our lusterless own.
  Ø
Drought has packed my anger so hard
that when it *does* rain, the water just runs off.

**Aggression Cue 9: Shouting.**

From correspondence in behavior one may postulate
commonalities of etiology and neurobiological mechanism.
Aggressive behaviors of humans display continuities with those
of nonhuman primates. Monkeys, too, fight over resources,
mates, and social status, in self-defense, and for protection
of kin, friends, sexual partners. Impulsive aggression in humans
parallels the poorly modulated aggression of certain monkeys.
  Ø
Necessity is the mother of resentment. No man can serve two angers.
Never repress until tomorrow what you can resent today.
  Ø
That's *not* what this is really about.
  Ø
Custom GTO. Liberty blue and parchment pearl, Ram Air IV,
factory four-speed, 455, factory buckets, rally gauges, Judge package.
Outta my way, mother fucker.
  Ø
Against popular culture's essentialist view — men are just violent,
men will be men — this study finds domestic violence one way
that batterers reconstruct men as masculine and women
as feminine, reproduce gender as dominance,
naturalize society's binary, hierarchical gender system.
  Ø
For a while you negotiate, but then you get even.
  Ø
Sapiens sapiens. Wise. Rational. Gods, not monkeys. Still,
a wire or two to the right spots and I'll turn your hostility
off and on like a closet light.
  Ø
(As when one spouse, perceiving aggression
from the other, behaves aggressively in return.)

**Aggression Cue 10: Encroachment upon personal space.**

Didn't recognize my anger when I dolled it up as courtesy, didja?
Cleans up real nice. Little black dress, eye liner, simple gold chain.
Smiles. Compliments the hostess. Flirts with her double-chinned husband.
But fuck that. And fuck you, too. Recognize it now?
  Ø
Once bitten, twice irate. One good turn deserves another.
  Ø
That's *not* what I agreed to.
  Ø
Officers on duty responded to commotion in the cell block —
hollering and lots of it. We seen smoke billowing
from the subject's cell. We seen the subject standing
in a pile of newspaper all afire, shouting "The whole world
is burning up!" Officers doused the fire, and moved the subject
to another cell, but even after the doctor come, he kept on:
"Fire! Fire! Everything is on fire!"
  Ø
For a while you get pushed around, but then you push back.
  Ø
I've got a family to feed, a cause to defend.
  Ø
I will not be afraid of how fast things are changing around me.
I will not be afraid of how fast things are changing around me.
I will not be afraid of how fast things are changing around me.
I will not be afraid of how fast everything changes all the time.
I will not be afraid of how fast things are changing around me.
I will not be angry at how fast things are changing around me.
  Ø
My anger *brags* about how many days in a row
it has parched now in hundred-degree heat.

**Aggression Cue 11: The stationing of troops.**

Bought this heap of crap for the bumper stickers.  Saw it
in the lot at Safeway.  Sweet Aussie — pretty markings —
in the rusted-out bed, intent on the store's automatic doors.
Truck means nothin to me but listen to this: *Screw Jane Fonda!*
*What has war ever done but end Nazism, communism, and slavery?*
*When in doubt, empty the magazine! A dead enemy is a peaceful enemy.*
*If you can read, thank a teacher.  If you can read English, thank a soldier.*
*Gun control = hitting your target.  In the ass-kicking business, business is good.*
     Ø
Penny nice and pound fuming.  Put your best fist forward.
     Ø
That's *not* gonna help.
     Ø
But who are the militia?  All the male inhabitants, sixteen to sixty;
all the knowledge and strength of the nation.
     Ø
That's an angry man walking his Rottweiler off leash.
That's an angry hummingbird buzzing my head over and over.
They sure are some angry raccoons this town's got.
Those are some angry sparrows.
     Ø
For a while you take orders, but then you throw a punch.
     Ø
Today we read from the cultural script called *Honor.*
Against any threat, I'd risk my life to defend yours,
but insult my mother and I'll kill you without remorse.
Only my readiness for *both* validates your trust.
Count on me no matter what, but don't tick me off.
     Ø
(As when one prisoner, perceiving aggression
from another, behaves aggressively in return.)

**Aggression Cue 12: Frequent interruption.**

Spare the rod, spoil the child.  Speak softly, and carry a big handgun.

    Ø

That's *not* where that belongs.

    Ø

The President lies because senators lie, and CEOs.  Gotta keep up.
I lie, you lie, we all lie for I lie.  Sports champions lie, head coaches,
ad agencies, corporate branding efforts.  Military dictators
in small countries that before the coup were called something else
lie, just like military dictators in big countries that have been big
since there were militaries and dictators, and the leaders of countries
that can afford to be smug because the people they victimize
live elsewhere and look different.  Spokespersons.  Pundits.
Middle managers.  School board members.  What the hell.

    Ø

For a while you play by the rules, but then you play to win.

    Ø

Were they the rural poor before we called them that?
Who got to choose the name?  Are they the rural stupid or the stupid poor?
Does anyone still bump an hour on a bus on gravel roads to get to school?

    Ø

I've got a family to feed, a fundamental right to defend.

    Ø

Had a dog once liked to get his way, would pay you back
if he didn't.  Tore up a cushion from the couch once
when he didn't get his walk on time.  Once he got
kicked off the bed, snuck back in later and took a shit
on a quilt my grandma made.  Angry dog that was.  *Angry* dog.

    Ø

It gets so cold at night here my anger freezes solid in the dog bowl.

**Aggression Cue 13: Use of expletives**.


Your house is burning and your year-old daughter is inside.
You don't need to know what started the fire,
you need to break down the door and get inside.
*But if I don't know to stay low and cover my face with a wet cloth,*
*I just pass out from smoke inhalation before I reach her, and we both die.*
You *think* too much.  You need to break down the damn door.
      Ø
To curse is human, to forgive asinine.  To the well-armed go the spoils.
      Ø
That's *not* the same thing.
      Ø
"Do you strongly agree, agree, disagree, or strongly disagree
that it is sometimes necessary to discipline a child
with a good, hard spanking?"  Percentages by Race and Gender.
"Do you think most children in America are physically safe
going to and from school, live in homes safe from violence,
live in safe neighborhoods, are safe from violence in the schools?"
Percentages by Young People and Parents.
      Ø
It's different now.  They *seem* angrier, and I *feel* angrier.
      Ø
You *think* too much.  Would it hurt you to *do* something?
Replace that worthless faucet, maybe?
Find one of those fucking terrorists you're so damn sweet on,
and kill him now *before* he hurts somebody?
      Ø
Hell hath no fury like mine, fucker, like mine.
      Ø
(As when one spectator, perceiving aggression
from another, behaves aggressively in return.)

**Aggression Cue 14: Breaking of fragile items**.

I drop things all the time.  If there were a world record
for broken bowls and broken stemware, I'd hold it.
Am I uncoordinated, or just angry?

   Ø

Wrath will out.  Where there's a weapon there's a way.
Wrath expands to kill the victims available.
Wrath is wasted on the young.

   Ø

That's *not* what caused the problem, and it's *not* going to solve it.

   Ø

What's interesting is *who* makes us angry and afraid.
Before, the state was the "us" threatened by "them."
"They" threatened "our" way of life, "our" government,
"our" institutions.  Now the state — that same government,
those institutions — is the "them" that threatens "us,"
against which "we" must unite, must take up arms.

   Ø

It's different now.  *They* used to be angrier, now *I* am.

   Ø

Stand still or you'll knock something over and break it.
Stand still too long, and you'll get knocked down.  Or knocked off.
Death, paralysis, guilt: an exhaustive list of the options.

   Ø

I've got a family to feed, a home to defend.

   Ø

When my anger *does* melt off the roof
the downspouts get so clogged with leaves and twigs
that it only drips at all the gutters' seams.

**Aggression Cue 15: Obscene gestures.**

Hell, yes, I'm high on the F-Scale.
People *can* be divided into the weak and the strong.
It *would* solve problems if we got rid of the freeloaders.
We *should* execute criminals and terrorists.
Kids *are* too lazy these days, and ungrateful to boot.
    Ø
You are what you shoot.
You're never too old to burn.
    Ø
That's *not* how things work around here.
    Ø
Boys get weapons, girls get dolls. Boys in rich countries
get toy weapons, everywhere else the weapons are real.
Everywhere else, girls have less time to play, after carrying water.
    Ø
It's different now. It's my *anger* that makes things make sense.
    Ø
Knew a man once liked to sit on his stoop and shoot
the starlings and sparrows. Right the hell in the city
this was, he coulda hit anybody passing by, and sometimes
the falling birds did. Angry man that was. *Angry* man.
    Ø
Cross-court winner. Strike, low and away. Ace.
Crackback block. Clothesline. Slam. Cheap shot.
Sucker punch. Pick six. Lights out.
    Ø
(As when one citizen, perceiving aggression
from another, behaves aggressively in return.)

## About the Author

H. L. Hix lives in a state whose self-defense law has replaced its "retreat rule," which required retreat if possible rather than killing an adversary, with a "true man rule" that allows a person to kill whether or not safe retreat is possible. The bill's sponsor included as part of her rationale the affirmation that "a man's home is his castle."

[This page intentionally left rancorous.]

# THE PLURAL OF *HATE SPEECH*

Think about whose anger is deemed honorable
and whose is deemed a threat.

## Preamble: Nomination Anthem

What shall we name the continuity between revolution and empire?
      Let us call it *American anger.*

What shall we name the dissonance between our pieties and our policies?
Between institutional ideality and practical reality?
      Let us call it *American anger.*

The irony of affirming imprisonment without cause, without recourse,
as necessary to our declared purpose of advancing human rights?
      Let us call it *American anger.*

The gap between the rhetoric of liberation and the practice of torture?
      Let us call it *American anger.*

What names the contradiction between our reverence for the
    "stay-at-home mom,"
the woman whose child-rearing is paid for by one man, and our scorn
for the "welfare mother," whose child-rearing is paid for by the community?
      What, if not *American anger*?

How might we speak of the tension between our professed commitment
to "liberty and justice for all" and the fact that the first forty-three persons
elected to the U.S. Presidency were white males?
      By speaking of *American anger.*

What would account for U.S. military spending
exceeding that of the next ten nations combined?
      What merits the name *American anger.*

For two million viewers, one hundred and twenty million dollars,
all to watch two grown men fight in a ring?  Five hundred million
in gross revenues to watch a few others fight in cages?
      *American anger, American anger.*

What do redistricting and voter photo i.d. laws have in common
with constitutional amendments prohibiting gay marriage?
        Let us call it *American anger*.

What trait does it figure that among us forty thousand people
buy and sell and breed and train pit bulls used in dogfighting?
        Nothing if not *American anger*.

How may we aptly designate the discrepancy between
our claim to collective sainthood — "one nation under God" —
and our assignment of others to an "axis of evil"?
        By calling it *American anger*.

**Days of 1852**

*Hartford Daily Times*, praising Samuel Colt
for the revolver: men of science can do
no greater service to humanity
than by adding to the efficiency
of warlike implements, so that the people
and nations may find stronger inducements
toward peace than naked moral suasion.


**Days of 1969**

"Stop shouting at one another": the advice
Nixon mustered in his inaugural address.
> *A carnival of anger has swept across*
> *every American metropolis.*
The leader of this mightiest of nations
dares not travel among its citizens.
> *A carnival of anger has swept across*
> *every American metropolis.*
Must we repeat empire's familiar theme,
violence abroad and repression at home?
> *A carnival of anger has swept across*
> *every American metropolis.*
An incipient civil war has begun.
Indivisible? Under God? One? Dream on.
> *Is it really others that pose the danger?*
> *Or we ourselves, our carnival of anger?*
It's safer to walk the streets of Saigon
than to walk the streets of Washington.

## Compromised Sonnet: Compromising Report

The immediate response was a wave of reprisals.
Was the site an arsenal because it was sacred,
or sacred because it was an arsenal?
The assassination that completed one conflict
started another.  What was the vengeance vengeance *for*?
The new leader has secured the old leader's compound.
It doesn't have to be declared to be a war.


## Compromised Sonnet: Compromising Declaration

Brown people there, brown people here,
brown people *from* there (where else?),
women, farmers, the homeless, the poor.
I am the leader of the free world,
I tell the snow where to fall.
*Le monde, c'est moi.*  If I am angry
with one, we are angry with them all.

**Compromised Sonnet: Compromising Inquest**

What features do I prefer in a killer?
Who has my permission to enact anger?
Am I the collected or the collector?
The colonized-by or the colonizer?
Do they not rhyme, pleasure/torture/other?
Who has, but does not use and enjoy, power?
What *did* I imagine happened in war?


**Compromised Sonnet: Compromising Assembly**

Five hundred, maybe six hundred other guys.
Egyptians, Arabic mostly.
It looked like what they did with the Japanese
after Pearl Harbor.  Lined us up.
The guards were screaming at us, cussing us out,
pushing around the oldest ones,
calling us bin Laden, stuff like that.

## Compromised Sonnet: Compromising Analysis

Push factors for transfer of industrial waste
from richer countries to poorer: "not in my back yard";
increasing regulation means increasing cost.
Pull factors: dump sites overseas charge less; they need
foreign exchange; regulations are less restrictive;
people there know less about its long-term effects.
Did I mention foreign is more cost-effective?


## Compromised Sonnet: Compromising Admonition

I was headed down to the subway
in Washington, D.C., when a man
grabbed my wrist and took my cane away.
He ordered me to *Move it, blind bitch.*
This was soon after the ADA.
He broke my cane. *Concentration camps,*
*that's where* all *you people ought to be.*

## Compromised Sonnet: Compromising Discipline

Some quarter-inch flexible plumbing line
works fine: it's a good spanking instrument.
It's light: it won't cause damage to the bone,
and can be carried, rolled up, in a pocket.
Ours are the same effective principles
that make any animal compliant:
the Amish use them to train stubborn mules.

Child rearing amounts to a test of wills.
Defiance will not go away on its own.
Verbal warnings are not parents' only tools.
*He that spareth the rod hateth his son.*
We won't give in: to stop applying the rod
would be to sacrifice our other views, on
human nature, love, eternity, God.

## Compromised Sonnet: Compromising Prophecy

At the Rapture, when millions of Americans,
the Bible believers, are called up to heaven,
suddenly America will be a third-world nation,
and Europe, where there are fewer Christians
to be raptured, will step in to dominate.
The EU, the rebirth of the Roman Empire,
will be the world power, led by the Antichrist.

## Torture Ghazal

First we were angry because we thought he was involved
with terrorism, then we were angry because we were wrong.

We had photographs. There he was, in broad daylight,
drinking coffee with a suspected terrorist. You'd be wrong

to think we had nothing to go on. Do *your* friends
have names like Maher Arar? Do they drink coffee with the wrong

sort of people? Yes, he was an engineer, but if you think
being evil also means being stupid, you're wrong.

He needed encouragement, so we gave him some. If you think
these people will talk because we ask politely, you're wrong.

We'd still have him if not for the damn Canadians
and their damn diplomats. Don't get me wrong,

their intentions are good. They're just naïve. They think
if we're nice, the bad guys will be, too. They're wrong

to think we can always play by the rules — that's exactly
what the terrorists count on. It's exactly how the wrong

team wins. Think of what they did to us. You'll be angry, too,
if it's right to suspect him, and just as angry if it's wrong.

## Hate Crime Legislation Couplet

1997, Georgia legislature, one demagogue:
"What's the big deal about a few swastikas on a synagogue?"

## "Get Tough" Sentencing and Prison Privatization Couplet

Less impunity,
more business opportunity.

## Invisible Punishment Couplet

Mere punishment for the original offense is not enough:
a convict's debt to society can never be paid off.

## Stealth Imperialism Couplet

America has "special global responsibilities":
we'll keep veto power, but we won't sign your treaties.


## God Hates Fags Couplet

Let me repeat, a massive homosexual revolution
can bring the judgement of God upon this nation.


## What's the Big Deal About Torture Couplet

An interrogation is not meant to be
a pleasant conversation over cakes and tea.

## Darwinian Rationale

Sea anemone, chimpanzee, crayfish, moorhen,
dark-eyed junco, African buffalo, human:

evolutionary advantage is conferred
by being the more formidable competitor.


## Impellors and Inhibitors: Cultural, Personal, Dyadic, Situational

Dispositional hostility, narcissism, testosterone,
target-specific jealousy, feelings of insecurity,
uncomfortable temperatures, violent media, physical pain.

Relationship commitment, relative physical size, sobriety,
plentiful cognitive processing time, sound executive function,
nondepleted self-regulatory resources, partner empathy.

## Aryan Nations Couplets

*They* are descendants of Cain, spawn of Eve's original sin,
her physical seduction by Satan.  *We* are the Children

of the Most High God.  Between us and them can never be
anything but perpetual war, natural enmity.


## What's Wrong With Kansas Stanzas

1938, Gerald B. Winrod:
if elected, I will use the office
of U.S. Senator as a sounding board
for the gospel of Jesus Chrise.

1996-2007, Jim Ryun:
YES to schools display "God Bless America,"
YES to marriage is one man one woman,
YES to school prayer during the war on terra.


## Background Checks Quatrain

Those Connecticut schoolchildren, sad story.
And their parents, tough luck.
But this is no time to make gun policy.
Everyone's all worked up.

**Futility Refrain**

*What? Am I shouting down a well here?*
Yes, dickhead, you are shouting down a well.

*What? Am I shouting down a well here?*
Yes, asshole, you are shouting down a well.

*What? Am I shouting down a well here?*
Yes, you stupid bastard, you are shouting down a well.

*What? Am I shouting down a well here?*
Yes, dumbfuck, you are shouting down a well.

*What am I shouting for? Why am I here?*
You tell me, shit-for-brains, you tell me.


**Bias-Crime Unit Sonnet**

Logs identify half the unit's cases as assault
and battery with a deadly weapon: with guns,
knives, baseball bats, motor vehicles.  In race-based cases,
in each year the weapon most commonly used
is the blunt instrument.  Here is one typical case:
a Black woman on the sidewalk passed a group
of six white men, who yelled such as *Nigger, go home*
and *Die, cunt*.  One then picked up a good-sized rock
and threw it, hitting her in the back.  For each type
of bias, at least half the cases were low-level crimes:
vandalism, threats, simple assault, harassment.
What is aforethought is *only* the malice.
Victims may be in the street, or in their own homes.

## Thomas Jefferson Couplet

I advance it as a suspicion only,
that blacks are inferior in mind and body.


## James Madison Couplet

Freed blacks should be removed beyond the region
occupied by a white population.


## George Washington Quatrains

They wash my linens, sew my shirts,
chop the wood for my fireplace,
powder my wig, polish my boots,
drive my carriage, saddle my horse,

serve my table, pour my wine,
light the lamps, post my letters,
plant the flowers in my garden,
trim the hedges, dust the furniture,

look after guests, plump my pillows,
sweep the porch, mop the floors,
make the beds, clean the windows,
perform myriad domestic chores.

### God Is On Our Side Statistic

Fundamentalist evangelicals are
more likely than the rest of the culture
to advocate state-sponsored warfare.

### Cynical Political Solution Quatrain

In the absence of consensus about what
would be, or how to build, a better society,
let's content ourselves with an easier substitute:
victory over an enemy, any enemy.

### Let's Not Kid Ourselves Quatrain

Offensive aggression distinguished from defensive:
it's not always guesswork to identify intent.
Note that the former is exquisitely sensitive
to the fighting capabilities of the opponent.

## Militias / Malicious / Mollitious

*Ditty #1: Ruby Ridge*

Freedom would be freedom to teach my children
Yahweh's laws and Yahweh's truth.  Don't need nobody,
don't want nobody, won't abide nobody on my mountain.
X
I've got kids just like he does.  I wouldn't want to be
the one to go in there having to point my gun
at a 10-year-old, knowing she would be shooting back at me.

*Ditty #2: Estes Park*

Of light and justice and liberty we few bear the torch.
To the forces of tyranny we will never yield.
To the drum from Valley Forge and Gettysburg we march.
X
You're wrong to think them *deviations* from American ideals.
Their question is not *which* ideals, but how much of each
we have, and how ideals are best defended and fulfilled.

*Ditty #3: The Minutemen*

You got your nigger Jews, your Asian Jews, your white Jews.
They're all Jews and they're all offspring of the Devil.
Turn a nigger inside out and you've got a Jew.
X
Communist infiltration at the highest level
of government made arming oneself, for DePugh,
as necessary as it made a coup inevitable.

*Ditty #4: The South Carolina Regulators, 1769*

Subsistence living rather than market production —
I mean hunting on public land, squatting, drifting —
such vagrancy makes you subject to our Regulation.
X

Regulators, then Moderators: only the threat of war forcing
consent to let the law take its course "without opposition,"
in place of escalating revenge, kidnapping, and flogging.

*Ditty #5: Gary Null*

This implanted transponder I.D. chip would replace
all currency. You would be constantly monitored.
It would control your access to travel or commerce.
      X
Their conspiracy theories find events in the world
folded, in full, into Biblical prophecies.
I wish *my* various mythologies so readily concurred.

*Ditty #6: Aryan Nations*

Eve's original sin, her physical seduction
by Satan, engendered Cain. In the world today
live his descendants, the literal children of Satan.
      X
It's God's law, not my rage, if I see things that way:
skin color as a marker of original sin,
sorting those who threaten from those who secure my soul's safety.

*Ditty #7: The Freemen*

LeRoy showed us the government isn't constitutional.
They foreclose on us to control the food supply.
He showed us how to fight for our farms. They'd like to kill us all.
      X
What does a farm couple do when they can't pay?
Go to the bank that told them to borrow enough capital
to keep up, only — this time — to be turned away.

*Ditty #8: William Pierce*

I wanted to kill the politicians and bureaucrats,
blow up government buildings, use a machine gun
to sweep the streets clean of all the non-Whites.
      X
But leaderless resistance, he claims now, will not bring down
the government.  For *effective* violence, he advocates
unity under a centralized organization.

*Ditty #9: Ruby Ridge*

The whole world lies in wickedness and we fight
spiritual battles.  We're gold, to be refined through fire.
We're anxious to get busy and can't really yet.
      X
It must be understood that Harris and Weaver
have been charged with felonies, and pose an immediate threat.
Every reasonable precaution will be taken.  However…

*Ditty #10: Posse Comitatus*

Why should we endure a lawless government?
Why forfeit self-defense, suffer violations of the law
that group action by neighbors with firearms could prevent?
      X
Spare the complications.  Give a man what he wants to know:
*Here's what you can do, and here's why God wants you to do it.*
No one can, no one will, forever take it on the jaw.

**Compromised Sonnet: Compromising Imperative**

*Fuck you*, it said, spelled out in foot-tall letters,
in cursive, in ketchup, on the kitchen floor.
No underline, no exclamation point.  Of course,
ants outlined it by the time I got home.
She had taken care to snap the squeeze bottle closed,
and return it to its spot in the refrigerator door.
Was there some way to read this, other than the one I chose?

**Compromised Sonnet: Compromising Prayer**

Unmoved mover, move over.  Meet Fever, my lover.
Former lover.  Red rover, red rover, let Lola
come over.  Love her now, all of her.  Most the low of her,
low that leavens my loafing loaf.  Fever fondled fine,
but I'd love to let Lola loose, let her make my loose change drop,
wrestle her and lose.  Fever, my forever, turned me out.
Turned out she loved me not.  Lemme give Lola a shot.

38

## Compromised Sonnet: Compromising List

Things that spread: crack in plaster,
crack in ice, crack in a windshield.
Arthritis. Obviously, cancer.
Snake uncoiling, line of ants.
The tuberculosis bacillus.
Beaten eggs across a skillet.
Mold in the yogurt. Bindweed. Crabgrass.


## Compromised Sonnet: Compromising Paean

I celebrate the cruelty of *practice*.
A toast to Mrs. Chryselephantine,
my first piano catechist, who smacked us,
her dimple-knuckled, leg-swinging charges,
up one diatonic and down the other.
*Don't leave this bench till you've moved all five pennies.*
I never played ball with my brother.

**Compromised Sonnet: Compromising Interview**

Have you ever intervened to prevent
the violence you are documenting?
Have you ever felt morally anguished
by photographing such great suffering?
How can you just stand there and watch?
*Is it* just *standing there, to stand there?*
*Is it* just *watching, to watch?*


**Compromised Sonnet: Compromising Estimation**

Tell me again why I should wash every glass.
Once around the rim, refill it with water,
no one will know the difference.  One quick pass
over a plate and it's ready for the next dish.
So I'm not Mr. Clean.  Since when are you?
America was built on profit margin, not soap.
You must have more time and money than I do.

## Compromised Sonnet: Compromising Complaint

If he's so all-fired upset over the shared room,
if no tv or phone and just a curtain between
herself and someone equally old and infirm
isn't good enough for his beloved mother,
maybe he could have come over once or twice
to listen to her talk to people who aren't there,
or help me lift her onto the pot and wipe her ass.


## Compromised Sonnet: Compromising Explanation

I point my anger at other anger to make it two,
though it precede any anger I would know to point it at.
First I was angry, then I was angry at you.
First water bubbled from the spring, then I drank it.
For every poison within me, three work from outside.
For every poison I drink, three soak through my skin.
Every poison I inhale becomes three in my blood.

**Police Brutality Limerick**

They took me downtown did the boys dressed in blue,
accused me of lifting a thing or two.
They treated me there
like the law's dancing bear.
Court is a circus that leads to the zoo.


**Survival Crimes Limerick**

Five from any thousand white women in prison.
*My jobs paid for shit, but I did feed my children.*
*Lock me away,*
*it's my kids who pay.*
Hispanic women, fifteen.  Black, thirty-seven.


**Short Anecdote in Which a Common Misconception About Anger Wins the Day**

Film Recovery Systems, 1986.  President,
plant manager, and foreman convicted of murder,
reckless conduct, and involuntary
manslaughter in the death of an employee
by cyanide poisoning in a plant
the prosecution called "a huge gas chamber."
The sentences, though, were overturned
on appeal, on the grounds
that the defendants' states of mind
did not warrant the convictions.

## Compromised Sonnet: Compromising Association

Anger and happiness merge, as brain functions.
Emotions organize around action tendencies:
fear and depression tend toward avoidance,
anger and happiness tend toward approach.
They share location: each sparks activity
in the orbital frontal cortex.  I am happiest
(as who is not?) when I am angry, angry, angry.


## Compromised Sonnet: Compromising Search

We shuffle our nouns like so many dominoes,
ignoring new combinations, new grammars, while we look
for just the right word.  Like a new one's gonna show,
like it's been here all the time, waiting to be found.
*Look, honey, here it is!* Truth.  Happiness.
Between the sofa cushions, behind the recliner.
All this time near our feet, or under our fat asses.

## Compromised Sonnet: Compromising Definition

*Ningaq* denotes physical aggression, or anger.
The Utku fear and forbid *ningaq* actions or feelings.
*Ningaq* thoughts are real and lethal: sooner or later,
the Utku believe, *ningaq* thoughts provoke *ningaq* deeds.
For an Utku adult, no situation justifies
*ningaq* feelings or behavior.  Toward no person
may *ningaq* be directed: no Utku, no one else.


## Compromised Sonnet: Compromising Suppositions

Grief, anger, fear, and anxiety
are frequently mentioned as causes,
but absence of explicit theory
and clearly defined methods leaves us
only primitive formulations,
nothing like systematic research.
Talk, talk, talk.  Violence, violence.

## Compromised Sonnet: Compromising Contrast

A subject with the trait we name *anger-in*
may recognize and acknowledge anger,
but inhibits all means of its expression:
verbal, physical, or any other.
An *anger-out* subject, though, expresses
in a verbal and/or physical manner
any anger he or she experiences.


## Compromised Sonnet: Compromising Debate

*Job*:
I kept trying to *account for* human misery,
but dark, loud God relieved me of that burden.
The lightning flash looked like it was outside me,
but the thunderclap felt like it was inside.

*Job's wife*:
Our children are dead, and the ass busies himself
with a theory.  Fuck you.  Fuck your ideas,
fuck your friends, fuck your talking thunderstorm.  I want *relief.*

## Compromised Sonnet: Compromising Rationalization

A violent man, like a ministry of defense,
will justify his violence with some version of
*I had to, I was provoked beyond endurance.*
No one else need listen; he'll tell it to himself.
*She kept nagging and nagging. She spends too much.*
*My Mother had dinner ready when Dad got home from work.*
*You could* tell *she was flirting with him, the bitch.*


## Compromised Sonnet: Compromising Profile

Subject lacks proper supervision.
Subject has a chip on his shoulder.
Subject needs more rigid discipline.
Subject does not show proper respect.
Recommend imposition of authority.
Recommend assignment to a juvenile home.
Recommend removal from polite society.

## American Ingenuity Villanelle

There've long been guns; there's *always* been the dream of multiple fire.
We put them together.  That dream became reality here

so we could fight as we fought when we fought against each other.
As long as there've been guns, gunmen have dreamed of multiple fire,

but Gatling, Maxim, Browning, Lewis all were American.
They made machine guns a fact of life; Henry Ford came later,

after our salesmen earned machine-gun pioneers their just reward.
As long as there've been guns, there's been the dream of multiple fire,
but the machine gun first became a reality here.


## Foreign Policy Villanelle

Hard power wins by force, soft power wins without coercion.
Smart power would win by applying *both*, in combination:

that's what it *means* to walk softly and carry a big, big stick.
Soft power is rare.  Hard power's means are easier to obtain:

we'd have to *earn* legitimacy, but we can *buy* weapons.
Smart power would be smart, but achieving the combination

is no easy feat: hard power assuages anger and fear.
Hard power embraces, soft power eschews, coercion.
Smart power — impossible dream! — would be their combination.

## Holding Cell Villanelle

Wouldn't fight for his country, yellow bastard.
Anyone who wants to bust him, go ahead.

The rest of us fought, but he thinks he's too good
to fight for our country, the yellow bastard.

I'm not saying how to treat him — you decide —
but anyone thinks he should bust him, go ahead.

Drink and smoke all day, I guess: God knows what he did
while we fought for our country. Yellow bastard
should learn his lesson. Want to bust him? Go ahead...


## Abortion Doctor Murder Villanelle

God's law is always more important than man's law.
I'm more relaxed now, and so is Wichita.

An unborn child is still a child, and all
God's children matter more than any human law.

I did what I did when I saw what I saw.
I'm more relaxed now, and so is Wichita.

For *their* future, we must act now. I won't allow
God's law to be corrupted by man's law.
I'm more relaxed now that I've helped Wichita.

## Paranoid Politics Villanelle

Felt persecution in, conspiracy theory out:
suspicious, aggressive, grandiose, apocalyptic, hot.

Paranoia as world-view, as a form of self-expression.
Felt persecution in, conspiracy theory out,

extremes as the norm, anger as the rule, not the exception.
Suspicious, aggressive, grandiose, apocalyptic, hot.

Paranoia in politics, like its clinical twin,
sucks persecution in, spits conspiracy theory out,
stays always suspicious, hostile, apocalyptic, hot.


## Sexual Violence Villanelle

Pursuit, precision, dominance, predation.
Toughness, immediacy, conquest, aggression.

Pornography has only a weak correlation
with sexual violence: dominance, predation.

What strongly correlates is the culture of the gun:
toughness, conquest, immediacy, aggression.

What makes a gun a gun also makes a man a man:
precision, dominance, pursuit, predation,
conquest, immediacy, toughness, aggression.

## Villanelle from the Case Files

Ken also has anger problems at home.
He has road rage, gets in fistfights sometimes.

He's only been at this job three months, but
already his boss is giving him problems.

*I don't play politics. If I'm upset,*
*I don't hide it from him. I don't play games.*

He reports that he has not, would never, hit
his wife, but does shove her around sometimes.

His heart races, his hands shake, his face feels hot,
his neck and shoulders tight. It feels the same,

no matter who he's angry at, or what about.
Ken has anger problems at work and at home.
He's put his fist through the wall a few times.

## Civilian Morale Villanelle

The military has a stake in civilian morale.
How curb dissent, with measures that are constitutional?

Modern war needs obedience at the front *and* behind the lines.
The military has a stake in civilian morale.

Think of Wilson silencing Wobblies: raids, arrests, convictions.
Nothing curbs dissent like the unconstitutional.

It *worked*: opposition weakens when its leaders are in jail.
The military has a stake in civilian morale.
How curb dissent, with measures that are constitutional?

## Crisis Orientation Villanelle

Violent behavior may become a *process addiction*
characterized by defensiveness, tunnel vision, projection.

First I hit her only when I had to; then, because I could.
Violence *feels better* when it is a process addiction:

guilt weakens over time, unlike frustration, which always builds
into defensiveness, tunnel vision, dependency, projection.

Don't fault my love for this intensity: yours is only cold.
*My* violent behavior became *her* process addiction.
Our defensiveness may look unwilled, but it's what we've chosen.

### Arrest Warrant Villanelle

Officer Jones uses last resorts as first steps.
Officer Jones takes pleasure in physical conquest.

He likes a good fight, with a worthy opponent.
He is a man who uses last resorts as first steps

to *take* respect when respect is not willingly lent.
He finds his greatest pleasure in physical conquest,

proving himself invulnerable, omnipotent.
His first principle is *in fistfights we trust*.
Officer Jones takes pleasure in last resorts.


### Ghetto Villanelle

The black kids and the white cops are strangely alike:
victims both, trapped in a conflict they didn't make

and can't control, can't keep from constant escalation.
The poor kids and the underpaid cops are alike,

their pride, their need to prove themselves, their isolation,
their fear and the desperate violence in its wake

that can't secure the respect it tries to insist on.
The black kids and the white cops are strangely alike:
victims of a conflict they themselves didn't make.

## Poverty Trap Villanelle

The poor do not awaken to breakfast,
or even have a place to shit and piss.

That job interview might be easier
for one who has enjoyed a hot breakfast

after a warm bed and a steaming shower,
or had at least a place to shit and piss.

Dressing for success cannot mask odor,
or compensate for having had no breakfast,
no bath, no private place to shit and piss.


## Psychopolitics Villanelle

Enemies should be cherished, cultivated, preserved.
Lose them, and our self-definition is endangered.

We are bound to those we love, *and* to those we hate.
Enemies should be cherished, cultivated, preserved.

"Good enough enemies" are only selves we've cast out.
Lose them, and our self-definition is endangered.

Without them for reservoirs, where store what we negate?
Enemies should be cherished, cultivated, preserved.
Lose them, and our self-definition is endangered.

## Gun Culture Villanelle

White, male, rural, Protestant, and middle-class.
My kid can kick your honor student's ass.

Demographics change; gun culture, though, remains
resolutely white, male, lower-middle-class.

Civilian gun stock: more guns in fewer homes,
the homes of kids who kick honor-student ass.

300 million firearms in private hands,
predominantly white, male, rural, middle-class,
anti-honor-student, pro-kicking-ass.


## Wartime Powers Villanelle

What do I trust my leaders *for*, if not to create
my Enemy a devil I can *see*?
War is a political *and* psychological state.

That was *my* slice of the pie that *He* just ate.
Nothing is the way it used to be.
I want someone to love; I need someone to hate.

We face a Beast, a Monster.  You can't negotiate
with Evil, with what lacks humanity.
War is a political *and* psychological state.
I want someone to love; I need someone to hate.

## Addendum: Bill of Slights

Ten (in)considerations, tokens of a longer list, even one indefinitely long:

1. "Manifest destiny" idealizes race hatred.

2. America's present pursuit of commercial and military control of others travesties its founding through revolution against imperial control.

3. There is, between our insistently reiterated conviction that we promote "ideals we share with all mankind" (JFK, 25 May 1961) and our paternalistic concern that others live in constant danger of having "alien ideals forced upon them" (JFK, same speech, same *sentence*), blatant contradiction.

4. Exceptionalism. The Greeks called it *hubris*.

5. Sound institutions would guarantee healthy practice only in a nation of flawless agents. The U.S. citizenry is not composed exclusively of flawless agents.

6. To regard the torture of other persons as justified is a *sign* of anger, but also a *form* of anger.

7. The injunction, perpetually broadcast in U.S. airports, to report to authorities any "suspicious behavior" by others enacts anger as paranoia.

8. *Don't pick fights, son, but don't EVER back down.*

9. Everybody knows by now that, notwithstanding the self-evidence of the equality of all, Thomas Jefferson owned slaves. But so did George Washington, James Madison, James Monroe, Andrew Jackson, and various other presidents and "founding fathers."

10. Nations in which capital punishment is outlawed: Argentina, Denmark, Georgia, Namibia, Uzbekistan. Nations in which capital punishment is still practiced: Afghanistan, China, North Korea, Saudi Arabia, the United States. Anger is *authorized* here, authorized and valorized and revered, in ways and to a degree that such alternatives as forgiveness and tolerance are not.

## About the Author

H. L. Hix lives in a state that, although in it occurred a murder notorious enough that the federal Hate Crime Prevention Act bears its victim's name, remains one of the five states in the union with no state hate-crimes legislation.

# THE ANGER CONSTRUCT

The inherent difficulty in defining the boundaries of the construct represents another challenge to future research on the etiology of aggression.

**Anger, considered by analogy with health and happiness:**

Socrates observes of health, Aristotle of happiness,
that it is a *state*, not a *feeling*.
I might *feel* healthy, but *be* unhealthy,
if for instance I am experiencing no symptoms yet
from the tumor growing in my left lung.
I might *feel* happy but *be* unhappy, if, say,
I have not learned yet that earlier today

my daughter died in a school bus accident.
We treat our anger, too, as a feeling,
but what if it's a state?
What if I need not *feel* angry at all, in order
to *be* angry, to be acting on — acting *out* — my anger?


**Anger, considered as a state:**

Suppose anger *is* state rather than feeling.  So what?
Feelings cease to be trustworthy guides, obviously.
But so, then, do *intentions*.  My being well-intentioned
will not establish that I'm not angry.  I might have only
best intentions toward my son, but be angry with him
for vandalizing his school.  Anger, in fact, might reveal
my well-intentionedness, my attempt to raise him well.

As a professor can bully a student, say, or a manager
an employee, not from intent to bully
but because the power relationships
supersede the intentions of any involved party,
so might I, without intending anger, be angry.

60

**Anger, regardless of affect:**

We don't define an act of violence as a "hate crime"
because the perpetrator describes himself as *feeling* hatred,
or understands himself as acting from a motive of hatred.
To the contrary, we would be surprised if that were true.
More likely, we think, the perpetrator will understand himself
as righteous: upholding justice, say, or purity
or honor, defending nation or family

or principle. Why, then, see an action as "angry"
only if the person performing it *feels* anger,
or would identify anger as its — his — motive?
Or recognize a person as angry only
if he recognizes himself as angry?


**Anger contrasted to hatred:**

Hatred is a *feeling*, anger a *state*. I *feel* hatred toward you,
but I *am* angry. It's a mistake to identify the two,
or to assume that the *condition* of anger
is always accompanied by the *feeling* of hatred.
The kindly white bus driver in 1950s Birmingham
may have *felt* goodwill toward the nice negroes
as they boarded, may have greeted regulars

by name, with a smile, commiserating about the heat.
He felt none of the hatred displayed
in Hazel Bryan's immortal rictus, but did his silently
watching passengers shuffle to the back of the bus
realize anger any less?

**Anger, not summative:**

We attribute anger typically to individuals.
Karen is nice to her father, we say, but all the time
angry at her mother.  Or, Karl ends up
in a bar brawl every week, it seems:
once he's drunk (he's always drunk), he gets so *angry*.
But what if groups, too, can be angry?  What if
that anger need not be summative?

What if, in other words, the group's anger is not merely
the sum of its members' personal angers?
Then group anger might cause, rather than
be caused by, the anger of an individual.
Or the two angers might be identical.


**Anger, considered in relation to groups:**

In case it seems strange to speak of *groups* as angry:
the John Birch Society, the Ku Klux Klan,
Bob Jones University, the Tea Party, the Black Panthers,
the Moral Majority, the Million Man March, United Steelworkers,
the crowd at a college football game when the coach
puts the starter in for another series after
his third interception, the furtive huddle at the water cooler.

What makes a group a group if *not* its anger?
PETA, Greenpeace, Moonies, Wal-Mart,
the North Carolina Citizen Militia, the IRA,
Fred Phelps's followers' children holding up their tags
assuring us that "God hates fags."

**Anger, considered in light of the word's etymology:**

"Anger" has an unusual etymology, apparently arriving in English
by two different paths from the same distant source.
On the one hand, it enters by the Old Norse *angra* (grieve, vex),
itself from the Old High German *engi* (narrow, painful).
On the other, it enters through the Latin *angere* (throttle, torment),
which comes from the Greek *agkhein*
(strangle). But both words, the Old High German

and the Greek, shadow the Proto-Indo-European base
*angh-* (tight, painfully constricted). All paths lead back,
then, to one origin: constriction, suffocation, binding.
One's own experience of it, tether.
Cuff, one's imposition of it on another.


**Anger, as in former days they spoke of it:**

Na man may to heven ga,
Bot-if he thole here anger and wa.
To suffren al þat god sente syknesses and angres.
Deliuer me from this anger þat I dwelle in.
In an angre toke he his swerde.
Anger is a vehement heat of the minde, which brings
palenesse to the countenance, burning

to the eyes, and trembling to the parts of the body.
Anger is uneasiness or discomposure
of the Mind upon the receit of any Injury,
with a present purpose of Revenge. The angry young men
run about shouting. Anger, that destroyer of our peace, that dæmon.

**Anger, by nomination:**

acrimony, agitation, aggravation, animosity, animus, annoyance, antagonism, antipathy, bad blood, berserk, bile, bitterness, black mood, blow up, cat fit, chagrin, choler, conniption, dander, disapprobation, displeasure, distemper, enmity, exasperation, excitement, ferocity, fierceness, fit, frenzy, fretfulness, fulmination, fury, gall, hatred, high dudgeon, hissy fit, hostility, hot blood, hot temper, huff, hysterics, ill humor, ill temper, impatience, impetuosity, indignation, infuriation, irascibility, ire, irritability,

irritation, malevolence, malice, malignity, miff, outrage, paddy, passion, peeve, petulance, pique, rage, rancor, rankling, resentment, savagery, slow burn, snit, soreness, spite, spleen, stew, storm, tantrum, temper, tempestuousness, tiff, turbulence, umbrage, vehemence, venomousness, vengeful fervency, vexation, vindictiveness, violence, wax, wrath, zealotry.


**Anger, by activation:**

acerbate, affront, aggravate, agitate, annoy, antagonize,
arouse, bait, blow up, boil, boil over, bristle, burn,
burn up, chafe, craze, cross, displease, drive into a rage,
egg on, embitter, enkindle, enrage, exacerbate,
exasperate, excite, fret, gall, get made,
get on one's nerves, get one's goat,
goad, incense, inflame, infuriate, irritate,

lose one's temper, madden, make bad blood, make one's blood boil,
make sore, miff, nettle, offend, outrage, pique, provoke,
put into a temper, put out of humor, raise hell, raise one's hackles,
rankle, rant, rave, rile, ruffle, seethe, steam, stew, stir up,
tempt, tee off, tick off, umbrage, vex, work up.

64

## Anger, by protestation:

Myne auenture heir tak will I, Quhethir it be eisfull or angry.
God had provided a severe and angry education to chastise
the frowardness of a young spirit.  Parys was moche angry
bycause he sawe wel that it was moche peryllous.
I am wroth and in my hert angry.
I'm angry, but my wrath will prove,
More Innocent than did thy Love.

Angry without daring to confess his resentment.
God was therefore angry upon them.  This busie, angry thing,
that scatters Discord.  Anger, which is a desire of revenge;
Hatred, which is anger inveterate.
I never ate with angrier appetite.


## Anger, considered as fundament:

We emphasize in the Declaration of Independence
the second paragraph, all that high-sounding bluster
about self-evident truths, our endowedness by
the capital C Creator with "certain unalienable Rights,"
praise of "Life, Liberty, and the pursuit of Happiness."
But read on.  After that, it manages mostly to grouse:
the King did this to us, the King did that to us.

What, after all that, is the first claim the colonies stake
upon declaring themselves "Free and Independent States"?
Not a right to be left in peace,
but that "they have full Power to levy War."
*This country is founded on anger.*

## Anger as rule rather than exception:

Massacres, enslavements, contaminations,
invasions, internments, persecutions, displacements.
We call them *events*, as if they happened of their own accord,
unaffected by our agency, never mind that we were there
for all of them. We keep dismissing them as *exceptions*.
We are a generous people, a people of goodwill,
committed to liberty and justice for all.

Any infelicities are temporary, anomalous, unintentional:
we had to, for their own good, to defend ourselves, to help others
who couldn't help themselves. But how many exceptions
can we claim? How consistent, how long, must this folderol
of exceptions be, before they become the rule?


## Anger, variously:

Anger's breadth appears in its susceptibility
to various prepositions. I am angry *at* her
for saying to me things I still can hardly believe she said.
I am angry *with* her friends
for helping her highlight my worst features.
I am angry *over* her adding up my small faults
to total a large guilt.

I am angry *about* the lies she still tells other people
to justify herself against me. I am angry *toward* those lies
for being closer to the truth than I would like.
I am angry *against* our friends who find
her story more credible than mine.

**Anger, all in a row:**

Anger is linear rather than cyclical. Traditional labeling of anger
as *sin* emphasizes the harm it does others. But it is *error*, too,
harming oneself along with others it touches. Compare it
with agriculture. Traditional agriculture is cyclical, employing
regenerative processes that sustain one another and in principle
may continue indefinitely; industrial agriculture demands inputs
of exhaustible resources (e.g. petroleum) and creates waste.

Similarly, wisdom is cyclical, maintaining regenerative
and reciprocal relationship with one's context, but anger,
by drawing down finite reserves (of patience, etc.)
and creating waste (of energy, of invective),
is ultimately both destructive of others and *self*-destructive.

**Anger, anger everywhere:**

To what is anger *not* connected?
In what am I not acting out my anger?
In what I eat? Not if feedlots and petroleum-derived fertilizer
count in evidence. In where I live?
Not if I trace back the sources of light
and heat in my home. In the car I drive? Not
if I take into account the wars fought

to keep oil cheap and flowing.
In the clothes I wear? Not if I consider
who made them and in what conditions.
In who I vote for? Not if I acknowledge how angry
I am at those angrier than me.

**Anger, that willful naiveté:**

Why do we insist that *this time* war will bring peace,
when all the evidence — all of history — says
it won't?  Anger may be *accompanied by* enflamed
negative feelings toward an antagonist, but it *is*
the mistaken premise that operational mastery
will eliminate conflict, that one party's submission
to another will relieve, not heighten, tension.

It is faith — naïve, absurd faith — in the equivalence,
even the identity, of military victory and political success.
Anger is first a false belief; only later does it become
a distressing, destructive feeling.  Anger is the illusion
that when my opponent cries *Uncle!* I've won.


**Anger, considered as a right:**

When the wealthy devalue the goods of the poor,
we call it fashion or market efficiency.  When the poor
devalue the goods of the wealthy, we call it vandalism.
If an adult displays anger toward a child, we call it discipline,
and we say a child is harmed who does not receive enough such anger.
If a child, though, displays anger toward an adult,
we call it a fit.

So, some advice:
if you're going to be angry,
be white, not black or brown.
The right to be angry is not distributed evenly.
First get rich, *then* get angry.

**Anger, epidemic:**

Any sound theory of anger must recognize
the perpetrators who populate prisons
as *symptoms*.  Focusing on those few who commit
what we name "murder" distracts us from recognizing
and addressing the structural causes of violent death
that end many more lives than the aberrations
we identify as criminal.  By "structural violence"

I mean the higher rates of death and disability
suffered by those lower on the social scale
than by those above them.  This higher level of suffering
is a function of class structure, not a whim of the Fates.
Behavioral violence is an anger tree; structural violence, the forest.


**Anger related to fear:**

*But what you're describing is* fear.  *People lash out when they're afraid.*
*Groups lash out when group members perceive the group or themselves*
*as threatened.  (And this perception need not be acknowledged: a white*
*supremacist's unwillingness to* admit *feeling threatened by blacks*
*doesn't mean he doesn't feel threatened.)*  Yes, of course,
anger is fear.  But no more than it is violence,
greed, lust, despair, hatred, prejudice, need, ignorance,

victimization, hunger, helplessness, hopelessness, aggression.
You're saying fear might *cause* anger,
and might be assuaged by it;
I'm saying anger is subsumed by fear, is but
one aspect or manifestation of it.

**Anger as response:**

Helen Block Lewis's shame-rage theory and Paul Gilbert's
social rank theory concur in describing anger as a defensive action.
In the one, self-concept concerns motivate anger;
in the other, concerns over status.  Lewis: feelings of shame
may instigate seething, hostile anger, a humiliated fury.  Gilbert:
shame may provoke assertion of status by strategic declaration
of agency and power through anger and aggression.

The one is synchronic: anger derives from situation.
The other is diachronic: anger results from evolution.
Both models describe anger as a response
to threats to ego and rank, not the result
merely of an angry temperament.

**Anger as animus:**

Firearms: physical realities, machines that propel bullets,
material objects that can be bought and sold, carried and fired.
Guns: totemic symbols, objects of fantasy,
ideas that can be imagined and desired.
This distinction shows us it's not firearms
we argue over: no one legislates for or against staplers,
or lobbies for or against toothpick dispensers.

We don't care about *firearms*, we care about *guns*.
The distinction makes visible an animus that begs to be named,
the animus that associates firearms with guns,
that replaces the physical machine with its semiotic brother.
Call that animus — what transforms firearm into gun — *anger*.

70

**Anger, synchronic and diachronic:**

Another distinction: *State anger* (*S-Anger*) is a temporary
psychobiological condition of elevated intensity of feeling —
from mild irritation to intense rage — with concomitant arousal
of the autonomic nervous system. *Trait anger* (*T-Anger*)
is an ongoing condition marked by propensity toward S-Anger.
T-Anger is fairly constant, S-Anger variable and occasional,
a function of circumstances (confrontation, injustice, verbal

or physical attack) and the subject's perception of them.
Persons with a high level of T-Anger perceive a wider range
of situations as occasions for S-Anger than do those low in T-Anger,
and consequently experience S-Anger more frequently
than others do, and more intensely.

**Anger less violent than pleasure:**

And what if I feel anger when I *am* an individual,
contentment or pleasure when I am not?
What if pleasure is the symptom of acquiescence,
the payoff from The System for complicity,
for participation in structural violence?
What if anger is less often and less
immediately a cause of violence than pleasure is?

What if anger signals that I do not concur with,
and will not abide, our ways of distributing
(*one for you, two for me*) the ingredients of well-being?
What if anger marks my refusal, not of the Good,
but of the way, and by whom, the Good is encoded?

**Anger, erasing its tracks:**

Incidents themselves manifest anger,
but so does the reporting of them.  Each gets
separate treatment, so that the mine disaster
can be construed as an *accident*, an "act of God,"
not a mass murder, the result of human greed,

human decisions.  School shooting here, bridge collapse there,
next up a heartwarming story: as *disconnected* events,
not elements that form a *pattern*.  It's a pleasing mode
of narration because it relieves me of responsibility,
obscures my complicity, reduces to an endless series
of entertaining dramas I can *observe* — shadows
on the cave wall — what is a unified problem I might *address*.

**Anger theorized, v. 1:**

But don't take my word for it, when we have
Martha Nussbaum's: "Anger is a reasonable
*type* of emotion to have, in a world
where it is reasonable to care deeply about
things that can be damaged by others.
The question about any given instance of anger
must then be, are the facts correct

and are the values balanced?... [I]f we try
to give a definition of an emotion such as anger…,
we will find, [Aristotle] suggests, that we cannot succeed in this task
if we mention only the way anger *feels*.… Anger
involves a belief about damage wrongfully inflicted."

**Anger theorized, v. 2:**

Or, from Sara Ahmed: "Your anger is
a judgment that something is wrong.
But in being heard as angry, your speech
is read as motivated by anger. Your anger
is read as unattributed, as if you are against x
because you are angry rather than being angry
because you are against x. You become angry

at the injustice of being heard as motivated by anger,
which makes it harder to separate yourself
from the object of your anger. You become entangled
with what you are angry about because you are
angry about how they have entangled you in your anger."


**Anger theorized, v. 3:**

Paul Woodruff: "[W]e should not want to wipe [anger] out,
but to bring [it] into harmony with reason."
And, "Anger is to injustice as pain is to injury.
If you do not notice pain, you may perish
through unnoticed injuries. If you are unable to suffer anger,
you may not recognize injustice,
and so be wiped out by the transgressions of others....

Our capacity for anger functions as our sensitivity to injustice.
Anger and justice are yoked.
An individual is just
insofar as his or her anger is keyed to injustice....
Learning to be angry better is part of acquiring justice...."

**Anger, easily mistaken:**

This anecdote points toward
(but is not itself exactly) what I mean.
When she was, what?, three or four,
one of my daughters complained to me
that her throat hurt, but it turned out
not to be a sore throat, just that she was about to vomit.
She was experiencing a symptom alright,

but she was *misinterpreting* it.
She *felt* something; she just didn't know what to *name* it.
She knew it was a symptom, but not what it was a symptom *of*.
She hadn't learned yet to connect that sensation
in her throat with an ailment in another organ.


**Anger as misattributed and misplaced frustration:**

Complex organisms such as mammals have evolved
to meet frustration with anger. Make this experiment:
place two rats on an electrified grid, and shock them.
They'll fight. Unable to identify the real enemy,
each will blame the other for pain that it can neither
interpret nor control. What pattern of action attends
stimulation of the lateral hypothalamus depends

wholly on context. It may be food hoarding,
retrieval of pups, or nest building, but it will be
agitated and intent. The brain cannot tell from internal cues
exactly what it wants, so it frequently misattributes frustration,
and misplaces the resulting aggression.

**Anger, anaesthetic:**

By analogy with "white noise" (*sensation* of which
has been gradually extinguished), some people
never "hear" the sound of their own anger.
Or again, by analogy with pain, one may distinguish
between *feeling* anger and *experiencing* anger.
Back when lobotomy was used to treat intractable pain,
patients, asked whether they were experiencing pain,

answered, surprisingly, "yes." Asked how they could sleep,
why they no longer cried out, they replied that,
though they still experienced pain, the pain was no longer painful.
In people angry enough for long enough, we see
extinction of sensation: *experience* of anger no longer *feels* angry.

**Anger variables:**

*Frequency.* Some people report feeling angry almost always;
others, almost never. *Intensity.* Mild (*agitation* or *annoyance*)
to very strong (*fury* or *rage*). *Duration.* Transient
or permanent (a grudge). *Associated behaviors.* Different people
express anger differently, with the result that various behaviors
(sulking, yelling, glaring, avoiding eye contact,
owning a home with a three-car garage, breach of contract…)

may be associated with a range of internal experiences.
The whole array (the many variables, the cognitive state
*and* the behaviors), not one particular internal feeling,
distinguishes anger from sadness, from anxiety…
Anger is a function of the whole person, the whole community.

## About the Author

H. L. Hix teaches at a university whose campus omphalos is a sculpture called "The University of Wyoming Family," which depicts a male figure and a female figure with a child. The stone from which it has been carved is white.

[This page intentionally left frustrated.]

## TWENTY LOVE SONGS AND A MEASURE OF DISDAIN

But it strikes, the hour of revenge, and I love you.

**Toxic Waste Love Song**

I would have assigned those cigarette burns to your forearms, my uranium
tailings love, had you not with those singe-stipples constellated yourself. {Ø} I
would have incised those scars along your slender wrists, my carbon monoxide
love. Permanence does not exclude delicacy. {Ø} Hand me that razor, my
acid rain love. Let *me* do that. {Ø} Which is stronger, my Exxon Valdez love,
my impulse to hurt you or yours to hurt yourself? {Ø} I hit you there, my BP
Deepwater Horizon love, from kindness, so that the bruises will not be visible to
others. {Ø} *Thus*, my CFC love, do I claim the insides of your thighs.


**Criminal Tendencies Love Song**

Keep the cheap piano but give me back my yellowed stack of unplayed sheet
music, my kleptomaniac love. {Ø} Return the 1985 calendar insurance agent
refrigerator magnet you took when you left me, my serial killer love. {Ø} That
you make your living with it now, my another week another bar brawl love,
doesn't make my custom two-piece pool cue yours.

## Carcinogens Love Song

Though I have not thrown you yet from a third-floor landing, my asbestos love, surely I should. {Ø} See how you like it, my radon love, if *I* in a fit throw shoes at *you*. {Ø} Don't think you're the only one, my tar and nicotine love, who can throw your grandmother's china against the kitchen cabinets. Already it was chipped from age and carelessness. Rage only hastens things. Your turn to duck. {Ø} Throw another punch at me and see, my vinyl chloride love, if I don't throw a harder one back.

## Alternatives To Rage: Candidate One: Posturing

Other species do the same: a threatened baboon
that stands its ground does not leap instantly
at the enemy's throat, but first enacts a series
of instinctive posturing actions, intimidating
but harmless, that present the posturer
as a dangerous, even deadly adversary.
Think of a bear threatening before it charges,
a dog growling, a gorilla thumping his chest.
Or, among humans, the plumed helmets
of Greek hoplites, the Rebel yell, gang members'
tattoos and jewelry and dress and gestures.

## Corporate Greed And Irresponsibility Love Song

If I could shit on you, my DuPont love, just the way birds shit their purple-stained shit all over my shiny car, I would. {∅} If only I were sure you'd shatter like crystal stemware, my Enron love, so I could drop you onto the hostess's hardwood. {∅} If I could tie you to a grocery cart and wheel it off a carrier's prow, my Halliburton love, I would. And wait and wait for the distant, barely audible splash. {∅} If only there were someone else as greedy and irresponsible as myself, my Lehman Brothers love, with whom I could contend for you as two hens will for a worm, tossing it and tugging it until they tear it in two. {∅} If I could pick at you I would, my AIG love, the way sparrows and starlings pick at a bruised and split windfall apple.


## Your Lyin' Eyes Love Song

You could become the *messenger* of my death, my iron pyrite love, only after having been its agent. {∅} Your promotion to management of my misery, my rose-tinted glasses love, recognizes your years of labor toward it. {∅} You could spend me on something useless and trivial, my full-page ad love, only because you first saved me up all those years. I have been to you like books of green stamps. {∅} There was, my spin doctor love, no point in offering me the razor until you had filled the bathtub for me. {∅} How quickly you changed, my sodium pentathol love, from receptionist handing me the clipboard of waiver forms to nurse practitioner swabbing my throat.

## Alternatives To Rage: Candidate Two: The Gisaro Ceremony

Against the pitch of this night many Kaluli crowd the bunks
of a longhouse.  Six tall boys with torches define the space
that suddenly four bodies painted black and red invade,
bodies plumed and jewelled, trailed by palm-leaf tails.
One at a time performs.  The first dancer's voice and limbs
conspire to draw the crowd toward their quietude.
His dance barely exceeds rocking, his song mumbling.
The song names recently deceased family and friends,
recounts events and places in their lives.  The lost return in —
return as — the rattle that merges the dancer's limbs and voice.
A weeping man leaps from one bunk, grabs a torch,
and whips the dancer's shoulders with its burning end,
which rouses from the bunks others who jump and shout and weep.
Their frenzied gestures and cries confirm the dancer's quiet
movement and song.  All is repeated at each dancer's turn.
It is best, they say, if the ceremony lasts until dawn,
and best if, during each song, many weep.

## Apocalyptic Endings Love Song

Our first night together, my asteroid colliding with earth love, I was thinking
the whole time of someone else. {Ø} I fantasize often about sexual adventures,
my alien invasion love, but the scenarios never include you. {Ø} Everyone's
subconscious is dominated by *someone*, my Yellowstone Caldera eruption love,
but I never awaken haunted by a dream of you. {Ø} I said *I do*, my nuclear
annihilation love, only because it was expected of me.  I didn't mean it even then.

## Pathogens Love Song

Come back, come back, my staphylococcus love. It's *my* turn to humiliate *you*. {Ø} Maybe time *would* heal all wounds, my rhinovirus love, but I prefer revenge. {Ø} Don't mistake my attitude toward you, my avian flu virus love. Don't take as indifference what in fact is disregard. {Ø} Though I knew my affection for you would fade over time, my mycobacterium love, I didn't expect it to turn so soon to scorn. {Ø} As much as I loved to fuck you then, my herpes simplex virus love, that's how much I love to hit you now. {Ø} Sssh, sssh. Ease yourself into the pain, my treponema pallidum spirochete love. I'm just getting started.


## Invasive Species Love Song

Let's see, my zebra mussel love, how much farther your fingers will bend back. {Ø} Let's test your arm to see how far it must be twisted before something — wrist, elbow, shoulder — gives. That sound, my kudzu love, will be erotic. {Ø} Just because I haven't yet doesn't mean I won't, my purple loosestrife love. Just because you want me to doesn't mean I will. {Ø} Just you wait, my water hyacinth love, just you wait. {Ø} What we have together, my Dutch Elm fungus love, is now, as it has been from the start, more corrupt than beautiful. {Ø} As are you, my mountain pine beetle love.

## Alternatives To Rage: Candidate Three: Sa-Salan

It's why the Kaluli sing:
to make themselves birds,
to make their words waterfalls,
to give those words interiors,
to be inside them together.
*Father, where are you going?*
Just when I have learned
to fill the forest, assayed
to shush the very stones.
*Father, where have you gone?*

## Collision Course Love Song

Keep your spite to yourself, my bumper car love, I have enough of my own. {Ø}
Just *listen* to yourself, my demolition derby love, the steam and cuss in what you
hiss at me, the cinders and grit in how you hiss it. {Ø} All this regret, my hit-
and-run love, yours for what was, and mine for what should have been, comes a
little late and for all its loitering matters not at all.

## Mass Starvation Love Song

With the patience of a vulture waiting for the coarse hyenas to finish, my Ethiopian Famine love. {Ø} With the presumption of the British royalty, my Irish Potato Famine love, the pretense of the Prime Minister. {Ø} With the inefficacy that lamed the Four Pests Campaign, the delusion that hobbled the whole Great Leap Forward, my Chinese Famine love. {Ø} With the ill-preparedness of the new government, the corruption of its newly-appointed officials, the new state's dearth of infrastructure, my Bangladesh Famine of 1974 love. {Ø} With Nazi disdain and indifference, my Dutch Hunger Winter love. {Ø} With denial and unnecessary delay and ineptitude that in other circumstances would be comical, even slapstick, my Bengal Famine love.

## Blood Sport Love Song

Allow yourself what law you will, my hare coursing love, still I and my sibling sighthound will win the chase. {Ø} I am Bad Newz, my dogfighting love. {Ø} I as satyr, my fox tossing love, you as nymph: nothing between us could stay between us, nothing between us could live.

**Alternatives To Rage: Candidate Four: Quiet Biting Attack**

Affective attack is marked by profound display of autonomic excitation:
piloerection, mydriasis, spitting, vocalization. Most commonly elicited
by stimuli that threaten the organism's survival, affective attack,
the behavior that evokes the term rage, is produced by stimulation
of the medial hypothalamus. The role of the amygdala is crucial:
stimulation of the medial amygdala can provoke displays of rage.
Quiet biting attack, in contrast, marked by stalking, pouncing,
and biting without autonomic activation, is elicited by stimulation
in the lateral hypothalamus. The two stand in inverse relationship:
the medial amygdala inhibits predation and facilitates rageful attack;
the ventral hippocampus facilitates predation and inhibits affective attack.
The one serves for defense when the environment threatens,
the other for predation when the environment permits.


**Numberless Casualties Love Song**

Don't fool yourself, my Second Punic War love, with the Fabian strategy. Small
skirmishes only keep me braced for bigger battles. {Ø} I've sent what tribute I'll
send, my Mongol Conquests love. Invade again if you must, if you think you
can. {Ø} Such a stench these corpses raise, my Gettysburg love, so many men, so
many horses, rotting under so hot a sun. {Ø} Someone, sometime would have
introduced the tank, my Battle of the Somme love. Why not us, why not now?
{Ø} I think before we knew anything else, my Siege of Leningrad love, we knew
this: that the Road of Life *just is* the Road of Death. {Ø} If we present them as
percentages, my Huaihai Campaign love, rather than in absolute numbers, maybe
our losses will not seem so steep. {Ø} Give me better names than Operation
Freedom Train and Operation Pocket Money for the series of futilities we are, my
Easter Offensive love.

**Devastating Journeys Love Song**

First snow, then snow on snow on snow, my Trail of Tears love, has enforced
on us these frostbitten feet. {Ø} I should have known no horse could survive
such conditions, my Scott's expedition to the South Pole love. {Ø} Never have
I killed so many hogs and cows, my Sherman's March love, cut down so much
corn, so much cotton. {Ø} Easier to orbit the earth a corpse than to return alive
from orbit, my Laika in Sputnik 2 love. {Ø} The cockpit voice recorder will give
no clues, my Pan Am Flight 103 love, and even eleven on the ground will die in
the debris.


**Celebrity Murderers Love Song**

Height improves aim, my Charles Whitman love, or anyway compensates for
it. From this vantage, with so many below, how could I miss? {Ø} What's the
difference between the cemetery and the landfill, my Bob Berdella love? Between
being buried in pieces and being buried whole? {Ø} Who could resist such
satisfaction now, *and* slaves in the afterlife, my Zodiac Killer love? {Ø} What
counts as care if not this, the saving of a skull, my Jeffrey Dahmer love? Who is
more attentive than me? {Ø} I can't get out of this attic, my Son of Sam love,
but from its window I watch you pass.


**Distance-Decay Function**

Assaults, for example: 47 percent take place
within half a mile of the offender's residence,
fully 70 percent within one mile. And "crimes
of passion" — homicide and rape — are
the most localized of all, often involving
perpetrators and victims from the same block,
even the same building. Which says what
about the dangers you face, my proximate love,
living with such as me, living with anyone at all.

**Cyborg Love Song**

The Geiger counter in your right arm should be alerting you to trouble, my
Six Million Dollar Man love, not from the heat but from the glow. {Ø}
Resistance would be futile, my Borg love, only if I feared the destroying myself
that accompanies — that *is* — the destroying you. {Ø} The inexorable logic
according to which your demise follows necessarily from mine appears to
you now, my Cyberwoman love, precisely *because* your emotional inhibitors
have failed. {Ø} You have things backward, my God Helmet love. My
interhemispheric intrusions are not *caused by*, but *cause*, disruption in your
vectorial hemisphericity. {Ø} That third ear attached now to your left arm,
my Stelarc love, should hear a ringing, high-pitched and constant. Take it as a
warning. {Ø} The faint red glow of your eyes, my Terminator love, sees less than
cosmic background radiation does, but learns more. Or will learn. Will learn
to shut down because I know how, and I will teach you. {Ø} The false memory
implant won't help. Your lifespan stays fixed, whether or not you believe yourself
human. Four years, my Replicant love. Four years, unless I end you first.


**Tables and Charts**

Figure 3: Five-year prevalence of each component of violence
by cohabitation/married status: Threat, Push, Slap, Choke,
Throw, Hit, Gun/knife, Kick, Beat, Sexual Assault.
Figure 7: Zero-order odds ratios for help-seeking behaviors
for separated relative to divorced victims: Confided in someone:
Family, Friend/neighbor, Co-worker, Lawyer, Clergy;
Visited doctor/nurse/hospital for treatment;
Contacted service provider: Crisis center, Counselor,
Community center, Shelter, Women's center.
Figure 9: Consequences of violence reported by victims:
Physical injury, Psychopathology, Altered psyche, Anger,
Time off everyday activities, Children witnessed violence.

## About the Author

H. L. Hix teaches at a university whose library owns the same number of copies of each Harry Potter book as it owns of a book by one of its own faculty members about the murder of one of its own students.

[This page intentionally left jingoistic.]

## ABSCESSIVE

I should be inclined to make the bones, rather than the heart, the seat of anger.

**I saved myself for** *this*?

Ornery he was, jess plain ornery. Wouldn nothin keep at boy quiet at school. Wouldn nothin keep him quiet in church. "Straighten up and fly right" is not a scolding he ever took a cotton to. If you shucked off all his anger, wouldn nothin be lefta him. Don't try to make sense of him or what he did. He was never *like* other boys. On him the prevailing wind was always blowin stiff toward crazy. I tried to raise him right, but they was always somethin in him I didn't put there. Call his mama a whore, tell him fish was bitin, didn matter. He'd still get mad. Never met anybody meanern him. Never figure to.

Don't know if he's angry,
but he sure is mean.

If your anger were a cave painting,
what would the figures be hunting?

A heavenly mansion,
raging in the dark.

But I don't *like* hominy.

"In the past 12 months,
how often would you say
you spanked or hit
your child(ren), kicked, bit,
or punched your child(ren),
hit or tried to hit your child
with something?" Percentage,
by Age, Sex, and Race of Parent,
and by Age of Children.
Percentage, by Income.

**I worked hard and saved up for *this*?**

That's just it, though, doc. Naming the problem *doesn't* help. We name and rename problems every time I come in. I can *list* the problems. My father fucked me early and often and hard. My mother knew but couldn't make him stop, and anyway she died when I was twelve. I smoke too much and drink *way* too much. I do self-destructive things when I drink, just like my father did. I *know* I smoke too much and drink too much, but I don't stop. I get in bad relationships with bad men, over and over. There are only bad men to get in relationships with. I'd rather have a bad relationship than no relationship at all. There are only bad relationships. I could go on. You know I could go on, and have plenty of times before. But I'm telling you *it doesn't help*. You keep assuring me that everyone else has similar problems, and I'm telling you *that doesn't help me*. You're offering to help me grieve over my problems, but I want you to fucking *fix* them.

Don't know if he's angry,
but I wouldn't want to find out.

If your anger were a car,
how many miles would it have on it?

Sing, goddess, the rage,
the consuming rage
of Achilles, son of Peleus…

Mama, Jimmy Lee threw my fish back,
and he won't stop laughin.

Stop-and-frisk. Him.
Stop-and-frisk. Her.
Stop-and-frisk. Him.

To reiterate,
the United States
did not in this case,
nor does it ever,
threaten criminal defendants
with designation
as enemy combatant
to obtain a guilty plea.

**I worked a second job all those years for *this*?**

Vulnerable Groups & Situations: Children.
Vulnerable Groups & Situations: Youth.
Vulnerable Groups & Situations: The Elderly.
Vulnerable Groups & Situations: Women.
Vulnerable Groups & Situations: Minorities.
Vulnerable Groups & Situations: Workers.
Vulnerable Groups & Situations: Rural Communities.
Vulnerable Groups & Situations: The Poor.
Vulnerable Groups & Situations: Immigrants.
Vulnerable Groups & Situations: The Infirm.

Don't know if he's angry,
but he sure likes to be in charge.

If your anger were on the lam,
what alias would it use?

My mood might be pensive, too,
if out my window I saw
daffodils, not shoreless, muddy,
pesticide-slicked floodwater.

If I come to an understanding
with the gradual decline,
will it hold, too, for the crash,
and for the sudden fall?
But I don't *like* grits.

I don't know what makes
for these disturbances,
but it's the same thing
that will bring on
the full-scale collapse.

Chill Penury repressed their noble rage.

Here we call it "The Hate Stare,"
that look you get if you ask
a white woman when's the bus
to Biloxi, or a white man
where's the men's room.

**I quit smoking and drinking for *this*?**

Recurring dream: I'm working at a quarry or strip mine, lugging stuff up the steep sides. It's heavy as rocks, but it's not rocks. People I know are there: my father, my best friend from school, my first wife, a regular crowd. They're just peering over the rim, watching. The other people working, I don't speak to or know. They look hungry and sick, but still *I'm* having trouble keeping up with *them*. There's a big explosion, and when I look toward it, two big pointing fingers of fire reach across the pit and take out my eyes.

Don't know if he's angry,
but I wouldn't let him
date my daughter.

If your anger were a lake,
how deep would it be?

Still another system may be affected:
the genito-urinary tract.
Anger is commonly involved
in erectile dysfunction,
frigidity, frequent urination.

The anger of Achilles, Peleus' son:
sing it, baby, sing devastation...

If I come to an understanding
with the deprivation, will it hold, too,
for the outrage, and for the assault?

Mama, Jimmy Lee took my pocket knife,
and he won't give it back.

NATO, yes, but
the State Department
is very much interested
in also getting
the corporate sector involved.
In a situation like this,
we need to work more closely
with the private sector.

**I risked my neck in those godforsaken jungles for *this*?**

Recurring dream: I'm driving my father's car. A motorcycle approaches in
the opposite lane. It's night, but I can see the road and the motorcycle and
its rider clearly, like you'd see them in daylight. I veer into the other lane, hit
the motorcycle, and its rider is thrown into my windshield. His head (he's not
wearing a helmet) breaks through the windshield but his body goes on over the
car, so he's decapitated, and his head falls to the floor of the car.

Don't know if he's angry,
but he sure likes to get his way.

If your anger were an eye,
how far could it see?

I'm glad we hooked up.
You were great.
I don't want to see you again,
but I wish I knew
how I could hook up more often.

You, to whom love was peace,
that now is rage.

"Power assurance rapists"
differ from "anger rapists."
"Anger rapists" differ
from "sadists,"
who differ in turn
from "organized rapists."
Each crime bears
a "signature" that declares
the personal meaning
of the rape for the rapist,
tells which cultural script
he was enacting.

But I don't *like* my okra cooked that way.

**I risked my neck in that godforsaken desert for *this*?**

Distinguish with me aggression from violence, thus: *aggression* occurs when
I see my interest or honor tied to coercing you to fulfill my aims, not your
own; *violence*, one possible outcome of aggression, resolves by physical force a
conflict between coercer and coerced. The distinction is not clean: Is the hunter
aggressive or violent who brings down a deer? Which describes one hurried
driver who passes another in rush-hour traffic? Still, a distinction explains the
attraction of violence: mastery of one's environment is one thing, but mastery *by
inflicting pain* something else, more *intimate*.

Don't know if he's angry,
but he sure does order her around.

All anger, all the time: Peleus' son,
Achilles, goddess-sung…

Mama, Jimmy Lee's down nere in na
    shed
an it's all tore up.

If your anger were a sea,
what would swim in its depths?

If I come to an understanding
with the fungus, will it hold, too,
for the stain, and for the staph
    infection?

Homicide Rates, by Weapon,
Race, and Gender of Victim.
Rape Rates, by Race
and Gender of Victim.
Assault Rates, by Race
and Age of Victim,
and by Type of Assault.

**I risked my neck in those godforsaken mountains for *this*?**

If only they'd stolen a hundred jumbo jets full of Talmudic khazar mamzers, criminal regimeist whiggers, niggers, and the rest, and crashed them into the Supreme Court, the FBI building, Congress, all the state capitals, tv stations… *That* would have been a damn good start. Anyone willing to fly a plane into a building to kill Jews is alright by me. The enemy of our enemy is our friend. I wish our members had as much testicular fortitude.

Don't know if he's angry,
but he sure does talk a lot.

But I don't *like* the stupid gewgaws
you bring me back from your trips.

A furious, directed attack
against the enemy.
A furious, directed attack
against a bystander.
A furious, directed attack
against a symbol.
A furious, directed attack
against his own son.
A furious, directed attack
against his own father.

If your anger were a letter,
to whom would it be addressed?

Goddess, sing us
the overwhelming wrath
of Achilles, son of Peleus…

If I come to an understanding
with the fistfight, will it hold, too,
for the mine and the shelling?
Will it hold for the sniper fire?

I can stop the guy stalking my daughter,
but not the one stalking my wife.

I know I'm supposed to love best
those I know best,
and know best the one I love,
but what satisfaction
is there in finishing
someone else's sentences?

**I listened and took notes, for *this*?**

Then experimental psychologists made the useful distinction between a man who joins others to burn crosses near the homes of those with darker skins ("hostile aggression") and one who joins with others to preserve the exclusivity of a country club's membership ("instrumental aggression").

Don't know if he's angry,
but that's a lot of camo gear.

If your anger were a figure of speech,
into what languages would it be
impossible to translate?

I'll find you.  If you leave me,
I'll find you and kill you.

I tipped up anger, as a curious child
might tip up a stone half as heavy
as herself, and found beneath it
teeming fear, as she found
the moist soil seething
with insects and centipedes.

Mama, Jimmy Lee burnt down na shed.

Maybe not, but at least
it proves we still got
some balls in this country.

God's holy WHITE people
are commanded to arm themselves
against all non-whites
and all WHITE traitors.
REMEMBER
you are God's people and
GOD COMMANDS YOU TO KILL.

And barren rage of death's eternal cold.

Yes, but people *with* guns
kill people more often
than people without guns do.

**I put myself through school for** *this?*

For instance, a man who shoots his wife's lover might be assumed to be showing "hostile aggression," while a man who in robbing a bank shoots a teller to limit the number of witnesses in case he gets caught might be said to enact "instrumental aggression." Though often it *is* a man, it need not be. Three teenage girls who beat another as a ritual of gang initiation show "hostile aggression," while a woman who kills a man to prevent his continuing to rape her daughter enacts "instrumental aggression."

Don't know if he's angry,
but he sure does yell at those kids.

If your anger were a delegation,
who would it be representing,
with whom would it seek audience,
and what would it be tasked to say?

I tipped up fear, as a curious child
might tip up a stone half as heavy
as himself, and found beneath it
teeming anger, as he found the mud
animate with worms and arthropods.

Hate Crime Investigations,
by Category.
Hate Crime Investigations,
by Race of Victim.
Hate Crime Investigations,
by Race of Perpetrator.

But I don't *like* attracting
all those frantic sparrows to the yard,
as if there weren't plenty
frazzling it already.

Angry, he is angry, Peleus' son,
Achilles, with an anger
worth a goddess' song…

Fat people are stupid people,
and I shouldn't be fat
because I'm not stupid.
But fat people are also angry,
at themselves and at the world,
and I'm nothing if not angry.

The most reliable predictor
of aggressive political action,
its most frequent and proximal
emotional antecedent.

**All those committee meetings, for *this*?**

The distinction might be extended to groups. An organization that sponsors suicide bombings to avenge perceived injustice displays "hostile aggression," but a coalition that ousts an oppressive regime to secure a resource flow shows "instrumental aggression."

Don't know if he's angry,
but he sure is jumpy.

Start naming what drifts down,
the list gets long fast: feathers,
leaves, lint, seeds, pollen...
Always something, if only dust,
to receive it, to consume it.
Ashes, ashes, we all fall down.

Fury from Achilles, son of Peleus.
Goddess, sing how furious...

Your anger: thunderstorm, or mudslide?

Don't matter to me *how* long
Jimmy Lee's in prison for.

High explicit self-esteem
+ low implicit self-esteem
= violent.

You say what we *can* imagine
is what feeds our anger.
I say what we *cannot*.

Organizations —
think corporations,
think grey flannel suits —
stimulate camouflaged aggression
by mediating conflicts
through formal structures
and formalized procedures
that offer weapons and masks
for the delivery of aggression.

**I saved up all my sick days for *this*?**

Maybe the anger I hear in your words is anger I'd feel, too, in your place. Maybe it's the anger I feel already in mine. Or the anger I heard in the crowd at the rally, in the testimony of the accused. Hear, really, everywhere. Call it "righteous indignation" if you want, but it sounds like anger to me. Call it "freedom" but it still sounds like anger.

Don't know if he's angry,
but I know he gets *Guns & Ammo*.

If your anger were able
to assign names, what would it call
the resurfacing of a loon after a dive?

But I don't *like*
your goddam Christmas music.

Over my dead body.
Make my day.
You first.
That's what you said last time.
Beat *that*.
Your mama.
*Try* it. Just try it.
Shit.

Rage. Sing, goddess, of Peleus' son
Achilles, his outrageous rage…

Strongly agree. Agree.
No opinion. Disagree.
Strongly disagree.
"Welfare does more harm
than good, because
it breaks up the family
and weakens the work ethic."

Unfortunately, this way of coping
mostly gives distraction, but does not
address, much less solve,
the anger-causing situation.

Are *any* dreams my own?
Is any anger not?

**I stood in line all that time for *this*?**

Stuff takes over. Can't kill it, mint. It's pretty, but watch out. Anything can stand for anything else, for a little while. Women who embroider songbirds, women who knit mittens. Nobody makes lace by hand any more. Who would go to the trouble? Who still knows how? Even in a list of lost arts it would just get lost again. With doilies. Who *thought* of them? Who made the first one? I love the word, though. *Doilies, doilies, doilies.* Small doilies on each arm of grandma's easy chair, big doily on the back. I outlasted her, but she had a headstart and I'm catching up. She was wild when she was young. Hard to believe now. Pretty, they said, but watch out. *How does that happen, that something stops being useful or beautiful?* My grandmother's cousin knitted this trivet. I serve stuff straight off the stove, though, so I use it for a dishrag.

Don't know if he's angry,
but he sure likes to pick fights.

Don't ask *me* to do your dirty work.
Yeah, right.
On *what* planet?
Try again.
Just you wait and see.
*Fuck* you. Fuck *you.*
And don't come back.

If your anger were a billboard,
what would it advertise?

Mama, Jimmy Lee never *did*
come home last night.

Welcome to the new geography
of conflict, marked out
not by political boundaries
but by resource concentrations.
*Who's in charge here?* is so *Eisenhower.*
Repeat after me: *Where's the water?*
*Where's the oil? Outta my way.*

You're worried about
what they did to us,
I'm worried about
what we're doing to ourselves.
*They* don't scare me,
*we* scare me.

That old perplexity an empty purse.

**I worked out five days a week for *this*?**

Speaking of things to give up, how about romanticism? All those bird-blustery poets aswoon over skylarks and nightingales and cheerful serfs — beautiful girl serfs, of course — bending over sickles. Whistling and singing all the time, all the time a light breeze to carry it this way. You boys' world doesn't sound much like mine. I keep eyeing the field for a maiden, but that looks like a line of combines. And listening for a nightingale, not the godawful screams of those famished seagulls hassling them.

Don't know if he's angry,
but he sure is nervous.

But I don't *like*
your new subdivisions,
all those three-car garages
on look-alike houses
stapled together
under pasteboard siding.

Our study suggests
that women decide
very carefully when
and to whom
and in relation to what
they express anger, and that
they do so on *ethical*,
not strictly prudential, grounds.

The lion roars at the enraging desert.

Your anger: folding chair, or elevator?

Let's stick to passive forms
here, speaking only
of the women and children
who have been beaten,
raped, and killed,
not of the beating,
raping, and killing itself,
and certainly not of the men,
many of them husbands,
or of the boys, who do
the beating, raping, and killing.

Does it matter that angry
rhymes with hungry?

**I paid the house note on time, month after month, for *this*?**

Missed Collection: Refuse carts must be placed at the curb by 7 a.m. on your
scheduled pickup day.  Carts shall be placed at the curb with the arrows on the
lid of the cart pointing toward the street.  If the receptacle is not placed properly
to allow for collection by the automated truck or if the cart is not placed prior to
the truck's arrival, the city shall be deemed to have provided service whether or
not the receptacle is emptied.

Don't know if he's angry,
but I do try to avoid him.

Let someone else disprove your lie
by asserting its opposite
or pointing out its contradictions.
I prefer to repeat your lie
in another context.
Except where you're at war,
your camo isn't camo.

Jimmy Lee never did *nuthin* around here.

Your anger: loose shingle,
or frayed electrical cord?

I'll be the man with no face,
you be the man with no limbs.
Embrace me, my love.

Voracious Achilles, Peleus-born.
Sing to us, goddess, of his devouring...

If I come to an understanding
with the woodrot, will it hold, too,
for the cut, and for the explosion?

The day I was born
I was mad at somebody.
In 1970, from a Marvin Cooley tape,
I found out who it was: the IRS.

**I solicited all those donations for all those worthy causes, for *this*?**

I tried to number my angers, but I lost count. I tried to name my angers, but they all look alike. I tried to separate my angers, but my god what a tangle. I tried to hide my angers, but they won't keep still. I tried and tried to count them, but each time there were more. Nothing about anger itself brings any one anger to an end. Nothing about anger itself sets my anger any bounds. Nothing keeps the list of my angers from being indefinitely long.

Don't know if he's angry,
but I know his truck is loud, loud, loud.

Percentage of Murders
and Aggravated Assaults
Involving a Firearm.
Percentage of Violent Crimes
in Which Firearms Were Used.
Percentage of Accidental Deaths
Caused by Firearms.
Percentage of Suicides
Committed Using Firearms.

Your anger: crowbar, or billy club?

But I don't *like* it
when we're all together.

Anger, sing anger. Sing, goddess,
the anger of Achilles. Sing the anger
of Peleus' son, the abominable anger…

Does that make sense,
attacking someone else
in order to attack
something within yourself,
and attacking someone
to whom you are attracted?
*I don't* have *to make sense.*
*I'll shove sense up your damn ass.*

Voices of anger,
I charge you, gather.
Voices of anger,
I charge you, assemble and speak.

**Every day I flossed, no exceptions, and for *this*?**

I keep thinking about what happened, replaying it over and over in my head,
I can't think of anything else except what caused the anger, can't hold anything
except the anger itself. It's as if I've been flooded with feeling, as if everything is
under water, *I'm* underwater, I can't swim, can't breathe, in my mind I curse the
other person, I plot revenge, I make crazy plans for getting even once and for all.

Don't know if he's angry,
but I see the NRA decal
on his back bumper.

I'd rather see a pile of dead kids
than a pile of my guns taken away.

*Fear* of crime, by the way,
does not track
actual *level* of crime,
but *does* track the percentage
of the local population that is black.
Black males are construed
as "symbolic assailants"
whose mere *presence*
heightens fear, regardless
of statistical frequency of crime.

Your anger: junkyard, or landfill?

Rage warps my clearest cry to witless agony.

Never seen nobody
get so mad as Jimmy Lee,
so fast, and over *nuthin*.

This is not *my* anger
we're talking about.
This is *ultimate* anger,
divine wrath, holy sword.
This is the last battle
before the final trumpet.
We won't defeat evil
by talking nice to it.
You got issues with that,
take 'em up with God.

I can stop the guy stealing my wallet,
but not the one stealing my keys.

**I put three kids through school for** *this*?

Any aggressive act can be characterized along each of the following dimensions: degree of hostile or agitated affect present, automaticity, degree to which the primary goal is to harm the victim and benefit the perpetrator, and degree to which consequences are considered.

Don't know if he's angry,
but his dog sure is skittish.

Your anger: target practice,
or leftist pamphleteering?

Fits of rage, to lose their sting,
must be carried to the extreme,
concentrated into the tip
of a finely filed knitting needle.
As anger is an act of imagination,
so is its release. It is *spiritual*
to see the puncture, and the blood.

Synonyms for *angry*,
#17: *criminogenic*.

But I don't *like* you
when you get this way.

Anger. Sing us, goddess,
of Achilles, Peleus' son,
to his anger given over...

If I come to an understanding
with the leverage, will it hold, too,
for the pistol shot, and the hammering?

Depends on what you think
the bottom line is.
You say save the precious
goddam spotted owls.
I say kill or be killed.

Now let's talk about the conditions
that might result in beheadings
and make videos of them
wildly popular. Let's consider
what they suggest about
how the political is figured today.

**I changed all those diapers for** *this*?

Hediger calls it simply "individual distance," the constant space maintained
in many flocking species between any two individuals.  Starlings, say, space
themselves evenly along a wire, by exactly the distance at which no two could
reach each other with their beaks.  Think of this space, with individual distance
for its radius, as a small, movable territory, maintained by the same behavior
mechanisms individuals in other species use to demarcate territory.

Don't know if he's angry,
but he sure leaves
lots of stuff in that yard.

You can't be
who you want to be
if you're afraid.  A gun
can *give* you safety,
and *symbolize* that safety.
Protecting your body,
and *knowing* it's protected,
is the best way
to liberate your mind,
your self, your soul.

Your anger: bar brawls,
or sleeping late on a weekday?

Yeah, he makes me mad, but Jimmy Lee
makes his own self madder.

Don't try to project shit onto *me*.
*You're* the one who's angry.

Processing patterns
in a hypothetical
romantic relationship
predicted violence in actual
romantic relationships.

**I cleaned up after him for twenty years for *this*?**

Like all paleontological findings, these statistics on interpersonal killing during the Pleistocene are not unequivocal. Skeletons never lie, but can mislead: a skull fracture that looks like a blow from a blunt instrument wielded by a fellow Australopithecine might archive instead a fall from a tree. Skeletons can keep secrets, too, never letting on about a drowning or a hanging or a spear through the heart.

Don't know if he's angry,
but I wouldn't want to be
alone in a room with him.

If the white lab coats
are figuring out the rules,
and the black robes
are making them up,
whose job is it to notice
exceptions? What clerk
inhabits what cramped carrel,
cataloging counterexamples?

The correct answer is:
(c) I told you so.

But I don't *like*
the asshole I work for.

Your anger: shout, or echo?

44 percent reported fantasies
of forcing a partner
to submit to sex acts.
11 percent reported fantasies
of torturing a sexual partner;
20 percent, of whipping
or beating a partner.
The corresponding percentages
in women: 10 percent, 1 percent, 0.
You tell me what this means.

If my anger really had started
as suddenly as it seemed to,
if it had only been *pro*voked
and not *e*voked, how could it
have lasted as long as it has?

### I came back with half a leg for *this*?

When? I'll tell you when. When I'm feeling tired or feeling overwhelmed, that's when. When they assign me too many cases but don't give me enough help. When others don't do their part, but the work still has to get done. When the situation is out of my control. When my husband or my son "forgets" something important. When I feel I'm being taken advantage of. When they keep adding work, even though I already have too much to do. When others try to tell me how to do my job. When they don't consult me before making decisions that affect me. When he just *lies*, which he does all the time.

Don't know if he's angry,
but that's a lot of guns
for one person to own.

Risk markers signalling
the pre-assault phase
include such pre-rape behaviors
as touching the woman
against her wishes, making
inappropriate sexual jokes,
hostile or aggressive speech,
and/or acceptance of violence.

No other love rivals
my love of my anger.
Don't try to pretend
you don't love yours.

Your anger: trotline, or condor
cresting the canyon on a thermal?

I can stop the guy taking my paycheck,
but not the one taking my job.

In those days the factory rules
specified how to *act*, not
what to *feel*. Be angry
or don't be angry, just
show up on time every day
and meet your quota.
For the workers, too,
even clashes with foremen
played out matter-of-factly:
just incidents, not
emotional landmarks.

[This page intentionally left hostile.]

## About the Author

H. L. Hix lives in "The Equality State," a state in which the wealthiest county has per capita personal income *eight times* that of the poorest.

[This page intentionally left open onto the void.]

## GOD'S BOUNTY

The God of love and the God of anger are required in order to have an Idea.

## God's Bounty, as Stalking and Shooting from Cover

In our first war with the Indians, God pleased to show us
the vanity of our military skill, what infelicity attends
managing our arms after the European manner.
Now we are glad to learn the skulking way of war.
Our practice stalking venison for table shall secure us liberty,
their vanity, pursuing fox for sport, shall prove here
adequate only to defeat.  Our rough ways shall stain,
most willingly, those elaborate courtesies with blood.


## God's Bounty, as Normalization of the Pistol

What had been, before the Civil War, a specialty weapon,
now was a familiar and widely distributed household item.
Colt Firearms: 130,000 .44-caliber revolvers,
and 260,000 other pistols made during the war.
Remington: 133,000 revolvers to the government.
The Starr Arms Company: 50,000 revolvers
delivered to the Ordnance Department by 1865.
Thousands more from Smith & Wesson and other companies.
Many no doubt rust unrecovered on muddy battlefields.
Still, that's a lot of practice, with a lot of weapons
returning in a lot of bedrolls to a lot of households.

## God's Bounty, as Abundance and Ready Availability of Matériel

Rammers, sponges, worms and ladles, with or without spring worms, ready covered, of all sizes, of superior quality • Copper gun ladles and double worms for every bore • Gunner's handspikes, plain or shod, and crowbars • Windlass and capstern handspikes • Best saltpetre and common match rope • Cannon priming horns, with screw bottoms • Cannon priming wires, bitts and augers • Lint-stocks, port-fire and false-fire stocks • Boarding pikes ready fitted, cutlasses and poll-axes • Musket's and pistol's • Musket and pistol balls and cartridges, with or without buck shot, either empty or filled • Musket cartridges in blank, for the exercise of the militia • Round, grape, canister, partridge, star, sliding gunter and langridge shot, either loose or quilted • Stools and bags for langridge and grape shot, of all sizes • Shot, cartridge and wad, formers & guages • Cannon cartridges, ready made to every bore • Cannon, musket cartridge and log book paper • Gun aprons, either lead or canvass • Tompions and port taugles • Sheep-skins for sponges, ready dressed • Musket, cannon and pistol powder & flints • Cannon provers, tryers, searchers and relievers, to discover any defect in the bore • Magazine, side, battle, poop, tin and other lanthorns, with directions how to fix the magazine lanthorn to prevent accidents • Hand cuffs and leg shackles • Port fire, slow fire, quick match, flambeaux, stink pots, fire balls, carcases, and composition for signals for convoys made up, of every description, & every species of fire work prepared at the shortest notice • Fuzes, tubes and powder chests, with full instructions for fitting them for close quarters to prevent being boarded • Sky rockets and colors of every description for signals; also fire arrows • Hand grenadoes, filled and fused • Conductors for howitzers • Chambered carronades • Copper and other powder measures • Musket, pistol, and cannon cartridge formes for every bore • Budge barrels, ready fitted • Flannel cartridges, fixed with either round, grape or cannister shot • Gunners' spiking mallets and spiking irons • Wad, hooks and arm chests, &c. &c.

Cannon, swivels, howitzers and carronades bought and sold on commission.

Powder proved for any person desirous of knowing its strength or quality.

Ready money given for lead and military stores of every kind.

## God's Bounty, as Perpetual War

*As in the prior World Wars, we didn't pick the fight;*
*we're only finishing what others started.*

If we can just construe "the war on terror" as World War IV,
we reassure ourselves. *Anything* we do is validated
by the trope all Americans know from "our" decisive victories
in World Wars I and II, and "World War III," the Cold War.

*We've been here before, we know what we must do,*
*the justice of our righteous cause guarantees final victory.*

It invites federal authorities to exercise
wartime prerogatives, expanding the state's police powers,
and circumscribing (as dangerous and crippling) due process.
It offers a stock of convenient analogies (September 11
is like December 7), thus skirting awkward questions.

*As in the prior World Wars, we didn't pick the fight;*
*we're only finishing what others started.*

It endorses ever more militaristic policies,
and suppresses anxiety about such militarism
by placing blame for it always elsewhere: on bin Laden,
Al Qaeda, Hussein, the Baath Party, weapons of mass destruction,
radical Islam, terrorists, suspected terrorists, terrorist cells.

*We've been here before, we know what we must do,*
*the justice of our righteous cause guarantees final victory.*

**God's Bounty, as Data Sets on Firearms Use**

National Violent Death Reporting System.  General Social Survey.
National Traumatic Occupational Fatality Surveillance System.
International Classification of External Causes of Injury.
Uniform Crime Reporting Program: National Incident-Based Reporting System.

Uniform Crime Reporting Program: Monthly Return of Offenses Known to Police.
Census of Manufacturers.  Youth Risk Behavior Surveillance System.
Producer Price Index.  National Census of Fatal Occupation Injuries.
National Electronic Injury Surveillance System All Injury Program.

National Hospital Ambulatory Medical Care Survey.
National Vital Statistics System — Final Mortality Data.
Firearm Inquiry Statistics.  National Mortality Followback Survey.
Law Enforcement Officers Killed and Assaulted.  BATF Firearms Trace Data.

National Study of Private Ownership of Firearms in the U.S.
National Vital Statistics System — Current Mortality Sample.
Data Elements for Emergency Dept. Systems.  Survey of Gun Owners in the U.S.
Survey of State Procedures Related to Firearm Sales.

Survey of Occupational Injuries and Illnesses.
Annual Firearms Manufacturing and Exportation Report.
Census of State and Federal Correctional Facilities.
Uniform Crime Reporting Program: Supplemental Homicide Reports.

Arrestee Drug Abuse Monitoring: Gun Addendum.
Monitoring the Future.  National Crime Victimization Survey.
Youth Crime Gun Interdiction Initiative.  Federal Justice Statistics Program.
Federal Firearms Licensee List.  National Violence Against Women Survey.

## God's Bounty, as a Secure Border

Or consider the organization known as the Minutemen,
formed of volunteers who converge on the border
between Mexico and the southwestern U.S. to assist
federal officers in preventing undocumented immigration.
Minutemen volunteers typically are armed: frequently
they wear camouflage clothing and pistols in holsters.
Most are middle-aged white men who have driven
across several U.S. states in an RV to reach the border.
They own and use high-powered binoculars
as aids to vigilance in their contest with "illegals."
The patriotic narratives they embrace give meaning
to their racial identities and their investment in firearms,
which serve as mechanical extensions of their bodies,
at once toy and weapon, declaration and symbol.

# God's Bounty, as the Image of Desire Implicit in Images of Terror

*Breaker boys posed/paused in a Pennsylvania mine:*

It accentuates their eyes, the coal dust
blackening their faces.  Most of the boys smile.
All the hats and coats in which they are dressed
are black.  Their noses and mouths are smeared with coal.

{}

*Near the center of the image, one man stares hard at the camera:*

1937, Louisville flood:
white billboard family smiling, driving;
real black faces below, lined up for food.
The American Way, our standard of living.

{}

*Posed for a portrait in Hiroshima, soon after:*

The boy looks wary, frowning, brow tight, each hand
hidden in his knitted vest, leaning close
against his mother.  The woman looks resigned,
a lock of hair blown across her face.

{}

*The first hydrogen bomb, successfully detonated:*

With its palette ranging yellow through black-red,
its glow defining the horizon line,
it looks placid, a strangely brilliant sunset,
clouds layered like roofs of a Japanese shrine.

{}

*They're clean-shaven, the men taunting him as he walks to class:*

The black man looks straight ahead, leans forward.
The white men gathered to a gauntlet smile,
laugh, blow smoke.  One makes a thumbs-down gesture.
They wear button-downs; he wears a coat and tie.

{}

*The officers firing the water gun are not visible from this angle:*

Blurred by mist from blasting pressure hoses,
a crowd of lookers-on textures the storefronts.
The demonstrators (their skirts and blouses,
his shirt and overalls) are soaked.  They hold hands.

{}

*No matter how desperate her grief, her touch remains tender:*

That cord in four places, evenly spaced
down the body bag, one loop bloomed from each cinch,
gives the beauty here.  That, and the woman's face
that might be laughing.  The corpse, though: which end is which?

{}

*The lash bends back the head of the last in the line:*

Stripped to the waist, coffled by lengths of cloth
(their own shirts, torn into strips?) that tie their hands
behind their backs, their necks together, the wraith-
captives trail captors who are solid, burdened.

{}

*The bridge of his nose hosts one small sun:*

The soldier's left hand shields his eyes from the sun.
He sits, not far from two corpses, in dirt.
On one leg, his gun; on one hip, his canteen.
Nearby, a third corpse, implied by one bare foot.

{}

*Caps, epaulets, neat rows of buttons:*

One general, doubting-Thomas-like, touches
a bullet hole in the corpse's bare chest.
Another strokes his hair.  Though Guevara's eyes
match his smile, his hand is clenched in a fist.

{}

*She has a flower painted on her jeans:*

Of course the wailing woman's expression,
but also her posture: kneeling on one knee,
arms out.  And the posture of the fallen man:
prone, full-length, left forearm under his belly.

{}

*On the men's heads, metal; on the women's, cloth:*

Ten soldiers walk away from strewn debris.
Three women, carrying what they can, return.
A few buildings still stand, and a few trees.
Everyone is muddy, everyone looks down.

{}

*Both women wear jackets; the man wears short sleeves:*

The faces gaze each in its own direction.
The man looks away, fidgets, shrugs his shoulders.
One of the women concentrates, looking down
but not at the folded papers she holds.

{}

*Being albino does not protect a boy against hunger:*

Bent at the waist, one hand on a knee,
one hip and one elbow against a wall
to prop himself up, but insistently
holding what once held something edible.

{}

*The standing men form a row behind him:*

The crouching man's hair, like the pavement, is wet.
Still, the men have managed a fire. His gaze
points one way, his pistol another. That white
handkerchief insists *ghost* of his mouth, his nose.

{}

*So much drab makes the few white shirts or hats almost shine:*

How ladders that long and rickety bear
so many shoulders, so many sacks of rock,
God knows. Haze says the miners breathe dust, not air.
Those ladders say they weigh their words, if they speak.

{}

*The fence through which they pass the child looks makeshift:*

The boy's legs splay, slightly higher than his head,
the barbed wire has been pried apart, just enough.
Are the young arms receiving him, or the old?
To guard his hand, someone has pulled down his sleeve.

{}

*Each as if to protect the other:*

Whether the boy's wariness (that clenched fist)
or the kitten's (claws out) is more visceral.
Which expression most manifests mistrust.
Who, when each grows up, will prove more feral.

{}

*He bends at the waist to take off the stump near its roots:*

Nothing of this *after* defers to *before*.
Nothing recalls *canopy* to *clear-cut slope*.
Those distant wisps of cirrus do not prefer
old growth to new, rain forest to cash crop.

{}

*Of a million men, any three:*

Two look down, into the camera, one
up, out, beyond. One man wears a bowler,
a bow tie, glasses that double the skyline.
One man's hand rests on another's shoulder.

{}

128

*A time to build up, and a time to tear down:*

Sledgehammer poised.  One leg straight, the other
flexed.  Backlit into flatness, mere silhouette
against the hills behind, the rising water.
Still, you can see the shadow's cigarette.

{}

*It looks like a roll of packing tape he wears on his arm:*

Surely the two bullets had made him a corpse
already, before the *Carabinieri*
ran over him, and the gas-masked riot force
reclaimed the protester-breached territory.

{}

*The stretch of pavement all gritty, litter-strewn:*

Clustered figures, each clad head to foot in black,
fleeing the sources of thick smoke, a sky's worth.
In one's arms swaddling, on one's head a sack:
otherwise identical, death fleeing death.

{}          .

*It's black and thick, all that smoke behind her:*

That baby she carries at her shoulder:
his features, his expression repeat hers.
Is she the boy's sister, or his mother?
*To* what are they escaping, *from* those fires?

{}

*The mother's face creased, the others' expressions all hidden:*

One arm through the grate, hand clasping the boy's neck
to draw him closer, he and his sister
both shy, looking down.  Both women wear black.
Smudges hint handprint, pressed into plaster.

{}

*His fingers curl loosely, not in a fist:*

His left arm extends well past the stretcher,
an i.v. port at its elbow, taped down.
5676 written in black marker
on his forearm, matched in ballpoint on a wristband.

{}

*His face* looks *peaceful, at least:*

He might be napping on the stretcher, eyes closed,
mouth open, thin blanket of purple wool,
had not the nearby feet such rigid toes,
but for the blood, its floor-tile-segmented pool.

{}

*He looks older than the men rescuing him:*

He would look like a statue, the wounded man
being carried to help (expressionless face,
posture stiff), except blood starts at his chin
and has stained his shirt to the waist.

## About the Author

H. L. Hix has labored for some years to take on the character and responsibilities of a rational person and deliberative citizen, but one of his State Representatives would relieve him of that burden, declaring that "in Wyoming, we are common-sense folks."

[This page intentionally left complacent and self-satisfied.]

# ERINYENEUTICS

How should we read the signs of this rage?

## Fire, Venom

War the broker of bodies for gold,
who holds in his scales each battle,
    spits out of Ilium
    the fire-finalized,
ashes mudded with their brothers' tears,
borne in merest urns to their dearest.
The troops lament each with due praise,
one who was ever combat-ready,
one who fell fulfilling his valor,
lost to someone else's cause.
They mutter, though, under their breath,
venomous anger at Atreus' sons
slithering through their grief.
    Others buried next the wall
    forfeit their beauty to grave-
    vexed Ilium, erased by
    the very land they annexed.

## Wounds, Recklessness

The new order ensures
catastrophe, if
above justice it honors
the killer's cause.
This deed's sanction would recommend
recklessness to all.
Many such wounds
should parents expect
from their children then.

Then we who watch mortals
would not send our anger
to hound just the wrongdoer —
we'd loose death indiscriminately.
Though one see his own suffering
in another's, try to picture
when or how the tribulation
might end, yet no prescription
would remedy that ill.

## Horse, Girl

Attend justice and reverence:
become our advocate.  Do not
    betray the fugitive
driven by the godless
      into distant exile.

Let no one drag me away
from this the seat of many gods,
    you who rule this place:
consider the pride of men,
      remember their anger.

Do not watch idly while I your suppliant
am dragged from the statues despite all justice,
    a horse by its harness,
a girl by her delicate dress.

Know this: what you determine now for me
will in strict proportion
    return upon your children.
In your decision mime divine magnificence.

## Crop, Harvest

Though voiceless, these corpses heaped for all to see
warn even future generations that we mortals
hurry our mortality when we overreach.
Outrage, nurtured to full ripeness, bears
a crop of folly and a harvest of tears.
Look on the consequences these suffered.
Remember Athens and Greece. Do not,
overestimating others' estates, forfeit your own
present good to vain pursuit of another's goods.
Zeus will not ignore, nor does he indulge,
selfish ambition: he is a severe auditor.
Therefore offer Xerxes counsel of reason:
advise him to temper his brashness
with wisdom enough to avoid insult to the gods.


## Shriek, Shiver

Phoebus, dreamdealer to the house,
deep in the night out of sleep exhaled
anger as a shiver-sending shriek, a cry
from within that shook most severely
the women in the house.
    Readers of dreams
    under oath to the god
    declared it the wrath
    of those underground,
their grudge against their murderers.

## Fruit, Blood

Why so anxious, son?  Don't let righteous
indignation carry you off into folly.
Cast out at its birth this ill lust.

Since the deed is spurred forward by God,
let the whole line of Laius, detested by Phoebus,
enter the current of the River of Wailing.

Too stinging is the passion pushing you
to manslaughter, to taste the bitter fruit
that follows all shedding of blood.


## As Best, Until

But you, no novice, don't need me for teacher.
Protect yourself as best you know how.
I will embrace my present sentence,
until Zeus release himself from this anger.

138

## His Half, Your Half

His half of this argument seemed spoken
in anger, but so, Oedipus, did yours.
Enough.  We would better seek together
means of release from the curse of the god.


## Ever, When

They will not be my masters, *ever*.

Soon that will weigh on the Cadmeans.

What will make it so, my daughter?

Your anger, when your very grave exudes it.

## Flood, Wave

Do not carry in yourself one mind only,
as if your view, no other, could be right.
Who thinks himself alone possessed of judgment,
of eloquence, thinks no one else has reason,
is exposed by the unfolding of events.
One who has wisdom is not ashamed
to learn more, does not put up resistance.
You see, when rivers swell in flood season,
how pliant trees retain their branches,
but the unyielding ones are washed away.
So with a ship, if its commander insist
on full sail always, soon enough the mast
is underwater and the voyage over.
Yield your anger, permit yourself change.


## Hers, Yours

No more anger, by the gods! Each one's words
offer profit to the other, if you would learn
to heed her advice, and she to heed yours.

## Except, No Matter

Speak. I would be foolish not to listen.
I have among the Greeks no surer ally.

Then hear me. Here before the gods, do not
be ruthless, throwing out this man unburied.
Give over anger, conquer your hatred,
do not trample justice underfoot.
Once he was *my* greatest enemy, too,
when I won the armor of Achilles,
but though he was despicable to me,
I would not travesty his due honor
as (except Achilles) the most valiant man
among the Greeks who ventured to Troy.
To dishonor him would be unjust:
it would violate not him but divine law.
To injure a noble man after his death
is wrong, no matter how you hate him.


## Suspend, Rebut

Your pause gives me time to answer, Father,
so, despite your illness, hear me out.
What I request, it is just that you grant.
Suspend the anger that in you rouses
such fury, or you won't recognize as wrong
your urge for revenge, the anger you nurture.

You would rebut your rage, if you understood.

## Oaths, Inscription

What fortune the gods assign, good or ill,
a human cannot choose but accept.
But to those who cling to suffering
they have brought on themselves, it is wrong
to lend remorse or offer sympathy.
Your anger has made you a savage.
You refuse even well-spoken advice,
and declare its giver your enemy.
Still, I speak, with Zeus, god of oaths, for witness.
Mark my words, inscribe them in your memory.
Your illness was inflicted by the gods:
you dared approach the guardian of Chryse,
the snake that keeps hidden watch at the shrine.
So long as the sun rises in the east
and sets in the west, you will find no respite
from your misery, unless you go willingly
to Troy, to meet the sons of Asclepius,
who alone can release you from your rage.
*Then*, with your bow, with me as your ally,
with the whole world watching, will you topple Troy.

## Into, Against

Fierce the anger, malignant it grows,
when conflict thrusts friend against friend.


## Out Of, Away From

I, because of your calamity,
will measure out with tears
my dead life.  Suffering mother,
your labor pains were in vain.  Why?
I rage against the gods:
*Fuck you!  Fuck you!*
Conspiring Graces, why send this sufferer
who deserved no punishment
out of his country, far from his home?

143

## Into, Onto

Run, run, old men; away from the house
scatter.  Flee the man awakened into rage.
Soon piling new murders onto old
he'll frenzy this city of the Cadmeans.

Zeus, how can you hate him so, your own son?
Why launch him thus onto a sea of sufferings?

## Oracles, Dreams

O Phoebus, killing the monster made you lord
of the oracle, and now you occupy the golden seat,
from which throne of truth you deliver to mortals
divine wisdom issuing *out of* your sanctum by the springs
of Castalia, and *from* the very center of the earth.

But for displacing Themis,
daughter of Gaia herself,
from the holy seat, Earth in anger
began each night to issue phantoms,
dreams to haunt mortals' sleep,
revealing how things really stand,
and what events are destined.
Thus Earth from Phoebus
stole back the oracular office,
out of jealousy for her daughter.

## Ships, Horses

Menelaus, charged by erotic anger,
invoking the ancient oath to Tyndareus,
retained many Greeks to help avenge the wrong.
All Hellenes, then, will bent to his call,
assembled here at the strait of Aulis
their armaments: ships and shields, horses and chariots.

## Plea, Claim

Bury me, my mother, and you my sister,
in my homeland.  Turn back the city's anger,
assert my claim to just so much earth
from my birthplace, though I have lost my home.

## Earthen, Olympian

Hard hard anger
reveals of Pentheus
his earthen origin,
his birth from a dragon,
Echion, himself
of earthen nature,
fierce-faced monster, no mere mortal,
one of the giants who defied the gods.
He threatens to bind me,
devotee of Bromios, in tightest bonds,
as he has bound my comrades,
hiding them in prison darkness.
Do you see, son of Zeus,
Dionysus, how your prophets
are oppressed by torture?
Come, my lord, down from Olympus,
bearing your golden thyrsus,
restrain the hubris of this bloody man.

**True, Bent**

Anger: the would-be reason-true, passion-bent toward vengeance.

**And, And**

Anger and fear and regret and lamentation and love and rivalry and envy and other such, do you not find them kinds of pain planted in one's very soul?

I do.

And don't we find them lush, too, with irresistible pleasures?

**Spirit, Dog**

But what if he thinks himself ill-treated? Is not his spirit seething and angry and belligerent against what seems unjust, willing to suffer through hunger and cold and all the rest, continuing to victory, not ceasing valiant actions until it wins or dies or, like a dog ordered to heel by a shepherd, is called off by reason?

## Banishment, Return

So Peisander and the other envoys from the Athenians in Samos on arriving in
Athens made to the assembled citizens their case, in sum that only by recalling
Alcibiades and turning away from democracy could they gain the King for their
ally and defeat the Peloponnesians. Many gave counterarguments on behalf
of democracy, and Alcibiades' enemies protested that it would be terrible to
sanction the return of one who flouted the laws. The Eumolpidae and Ceryces,
citing as the basis for his banishment the mysteries, invoked the gods against
his return. Peisander rebutted the various counterarguments and complaints,
asking each opponent what other hope of survival the city could claim (the
Peloponnesians having, at sea and on alert, a navy at least as large as their
own, having in their alliance more cities, and having support from the King
and Tissaphernes, while Athens was bankrupt) if the King were not persuaded
to switch sides. When they admitted that they saw no other hope, he spoke
decisively. "This won't happen, we won't win the King's trust, if we don't govern
more wisely, by making only the few our leaders and focusing more on our
survival than on the constitution. (Later we can change things, if we want.)
Alcibiades must return; he alone can see us through."

At first the people were angry over this proposed return to oligarchy, but with
Peisander's insistence that there was no other way to survive, their fear, abetted
by the fantasy of afterward reverting, led them to acquiesce.

## Demagogues, Sycophants

Thus, with partisan bickering increasing again, and the people pushed into opposition, the city broke out into continuous and sweeping disturbance. Demagogues and sycophants proliferated, young people embraced the most debased language; in sum, people forfeited to distractions their inheritance of sobriety. The same prolonged security that allowed wealth to accumulate also oversaw the withering of common cause and reciprocity.

## Risk, Grief

Achilles, possessed of a reckless nature, always did formidable deeds on behalf of friends, so, assuming the collective anger of the Hellenes, he avenged Patroclus and Antilochus. What he observed about friendship to Ajax of Telamon is important to note. When Ajax asked what deeds posed the greatest danger, Achilles replied, "Those done over friends." Asked then what actions were pleasant and easy, he gave the same answer. To Ajax's wonder that one deed could be both onerous and effortless, Achilles answered, "The risk I willingly incur in doing great deeds to honor friends ends my grief for them."

## Lashes, Luxury

Now we must ask also whether those who are vicious and enjoy shedding human blood are angry when they kill persons who have not injured them, and who they don't *believe* have injured them: for example, Apollodorus and Phalaris. This is not anger but ferocity: it does not harm in return for an injury, but is willing to receive injury in order to harm. It lashes and scars not as vengeance but as luxury. What ought we make of it? This evil originates in anger but transforms it, by such frequent and satisfying exercise that it forgets clemency and rejects any spirit of shared humanity, into cruelty. They say that Hannibal, seeing a ditch filled with human blood, exclaimed, "What a lovely sight!" How much more beautiful would he have found it had he filled a river or a lake! Is it any wonder you revel in this sight more than any other, since you were born to bloodshed and from infancy inured to murder? Fortune will attend your cruelty for twenty years, gratifying your eyes with such spectacles. You'll see them at Trasumene and Cannae and finally at your own city, Carthage. Not long ago Volesus, under deified Augustus the proconsul of Asia, after decapitating three hundred men in one day, swaggered among the corpses with an arrogant expression, as if he had performed a magnificent and noteworthy feat, exclaiming in Greek, "What a kingly deed!" What would he have done, had he *been* a king? This was not anger but a greater evil, incurable.

## Everything, Nothing

But when through labor and justice the Republic had grown, when great kings
had been defeated in war, rogue nations and vast populations forced to submit,
when Carthage, Rome's rival for empire, had been destroyed, when access
had been gained to all seas and all lands, Fortune turned harsh and began to
confound everything. Those who had borne lightly labors, perils, doubts, and
hardships found onerous and miserable the leisure and wealth they had envied
others. So first for money, then for empire, their lust increased; and these
became the source of all their injustices. For avarice subverted honesty, integrity,
and the other virtues of character; instead, it taught self-satisfaction and cruelty,
taught taking for granted the gods, making everything for sale. From ambition
many made themselves false, keeping one thing hidden in the breast but another
ready on the tongue, weighing friendships and rivalries not in themselves but
according to self-interest, and developing appearance in preference to character.
At first this spread slowly, and was sometimes punished; later, when it reached
epidemic, the state changed, and a government once premised on justice and
merit turned cruel and intolerable.

Once wealth became the criterion for honor and the source of celebrity,
authority, and power, virtue atrophied, poverty became shameful, and integrity
became an affront. Because of wealth, their youth were infected with luxury
and greed and self-satisfaction. They plundered, they squandered; they scorned
what was their own and coveted what others had; they equated modesty
and shamelessness, divine and human; in nothing did they value gravity or
moderation.

## Fog, Hunger

No passion so disturbs the clarity of our judgment as anger. No one would hesitate to punish with death a judge who condemned criminals out of anger; why then permit fathers and teachers while they are angry to flog and chastise children? That's not correction but vengeance. Chastisement replaces medication for children: would we tolerate an intemperate doctor who treated her patient with anger?

We ourselves would do well never to lay a hand on our servants in anger. While our pulse races and we feel emotion, let us delay the encounter; things will seem different, truly, once we have calmed and cooled; while passion rules, passion speaks, not we ourselves.

Like bodies seen through fog, faults seen through anger look larger. Let one who is hungry have food; but let one who would chastise have for it no hunger or thirst.

## Blood, Grapes

Anger, terrible counselor, sometimes persuaded them that divine compulsion made it necessary for the people to shed blood. That brought before their bloodthirsty eyes the vision of Isaiah, and they saw, and made their fanatical followers see, the meek Lamb converted into an inexorable avenger, descending from the pinnacle of Edom, proud in his manifold power, trampling the nations as the trampler tramples grapes in the press, holding up his robes, covered in blood to his thighs. Oh, no, my God! I am to be your minister. You are a God of peace; let my first virtue be meekness.

## Figures, Phrases

I have heard persons normally moderate in judgment raise their voices in a paroxysm of rage over minutiae: "Someone like that should have four bullets put into him." "People like that don't deserve to live." The disproportion between sin and sentence they seem not to notice.

They'll say: This is only a figure of speech. But the formulations employed, the everyday phrases, indicate else.

[This page intentionally left resentful.]

**About the Author**

H. L. Hix teaches at a university that first tenured an African-American female in 2006, that first adopted partner benefits in 2011, and whose graduate school in 2011-12 awarded 14 "Energy GAs" and 2 minority GAs, a university that in 2013 reported minority student enrollment of 10% and that in 2015 pursued its mission to "Expose students to ... the complexities of an interdependent world" and to "Nurture an environment that values and manifests diversity" by eliminating from its curriculum the "Global Awareness" and "Cultural Diversity in the US" requirements.

[This page intentionally left embittered and sullen.]

# LOST WAX

Anger can fill the gap between the promise of a
feeling and the feeling of a feeling.

**Why *can't* anger occasion the calculated rather than the rash?**

If he hadn't pulled a pistol, I might have let the whole thing go.
I'm a peaceful man, neighborly as the next guy,
but don't push me around and *don't* stick a gun in my face.
You *will* regret it. He must have thought I would back down,
say "Yes, sir" and slink away. Must have thought he could scare me.
But I'm not afraid of anything, and I kiss no one's ass.

It started as soon as he moved in a few doors down.
Before that, this trailer park was a nice place. Nice people
who kept to themselves. On days when it wasn't too steamy,
I could sit out on my front steps half the afternoon
and play a few tunes. Didn't have to compete with much
besides trucks on the highway, and even they turn soon to white noise.
He kept to himself, too, but his dog was a nuisance.
Whenever the man was home, he left that dog outside
in a little makeshift "yard" he'd squared off with flimsy fencing.
You know the kind: sagging orange plastic from a roll.
Probably found it beside the road somewhere.
He never gave that dog any exercise — you never saw
the two of them out for a walk. He just put her out
in that square no bigger than a baby's crib, and left her there.
I felt sorry for the poor dog, really. Who wouldn't have?
If that was how he treated her when anyone could see,
you had to wonder what he did other times. So I felt sorry,
just not sorry enough to put up with all that noise.

The dog was a beagle. Looked really old, all grizzled and stiff,
with a mechanical walk: must have had arthritis.
And her coat was scraggly. Not dirty or diseased, just worn out.
She wasn't barking *at* anything. I doubt she could see
well enough to be much interested in what passed by,
and she wasn't a watchdog, alerting him to prowlers.
The racket wasn't even barking, really: it was *baying*.
Not like a doberman or pit bull, a purposeful snarl
that starts as an r-r-r-r deep in the throat, and rises from there

into a *better-keep-back* bark. This was a sorrowful wail
not directed to anyone or as anything, just offered up
to the moon or the four winds. And relentless. Relentless.

At first I just went over to knock on his door and ask for
a little consideration, could he keep the dog inside sometimes?
He's got neighbors, people on shifts might be sleeping, that sort of thing.
That dog could raise the dead, and *did* raise at least my father's voice:
*You don't stick up for yourself, nobody gonna stick up for you.*
*Don't let no one take your money, don't let* no one *take your pride.*
I'm not a bully, I wasn't going to start anything,
but I wasn't *about* to let an asshole like him
push me around in my own home. A man's got a right
to a little peace and quiet. Anybody's dog might bark
once in a while, I wouldn't grouse about that, I like dogs,
what's not to like about something that can flush a pheasant
or help blind people cross busy streets or herd dumb-ass cows,
but this was all the time, howling and baying constantly,
and the bastard just left that dog outside like there wasn't
another soul around to be bothered by it,
like no one in that whole trailer park might be trying to sleep.
Somebody had to remind him of common courtesy.

He didn't take kindly to being reminded. All I did was state
the obvious — the dog was noisy, which he couldn't much deny
since she kept right on making that racket the whole time I stood there —
and tell him to have a little respect for his neighbors
and keep the dog inside. I'm telling you, I was Mr. Polite.

He was not. Told me to mind my own goddam business.
Which I assured him I was doing. Things went on from there.
He called me something I don't much appreciate being called,
I dared him to step outside and look me in the eye,
man to man, and say that again. That's when he pulled the gun.
Which must have been sitting right there by the door, on a table
or a shelf, or maybe the arm of a chair. God knows how many
that means he's got in there. One by the front door, one by the bed,

one by the sofa where he sits to watch tv.  He never stopped
looking at me, just reached down and grabbed that gun by the barrel
with his left hand so he could give the handle to his right.

There's a mental image that'll stick with you: big dude, big beard,
big biker belly stretching his armpit-stained t-shirt and pushing down his belt,
that one arm raised to point the gun at you, one hairy finger
on the trigger, that fat thumb pushing down the lever to cock it,
all in one smooth movement like he's done this a few times before.
Which maybe he had, but he wasn't going to do it
to me without consequences.  I gave ground then, but I knew
before I got back to my own place what price he would pay.

I already had everything I needed.  The mice out here
never let up.  Past my trailer it's all open field: setting out
a trap or two won't keep them away.  Even the stray cats
can't keep up.  You *have* to use poison to control the pests here.
It didn't take long.  I had to run to the store for dog treats,
but I can see his trailer from the kitchen window of mine,
so I know when his truck is there and when it's not, and all
I needed was a minute.  Somewhere there's a fancy dog
from a fancy breed that would turn down a treat, but not a hound,
not any hound *I* ever knew.  Shoulda seen the bastard's face.
Didn't look so tough with his arms hanging down, keys in one hand,
twelve-pack in the other, standing there, no gun to bully with,
piecing things together, learning he messed with the wrong person.

More things my father always said: *I'd rather be angry than smart,*
and my favorite, *If you're gonna take revenge, make it sweet.*
Never did much for either of us, all his for-shit advice
(look at this dump I live in, should have seen him when he died),
but for once, just that one moment, standing at my shitty kitchen window,
watching my shit-faced neighbor shit himself, it didn't seem half bad.

**Must anger be expressed immediately?**

I was afraid of him from the day we met.
You could *feel* his anger, you just knew it could simmer
only so long before it boiled over.
I couldn't have told you *how* this would happen
or quite *when*, but I knew from the first
*that* it would happen. That it had to.


**Does it have to look like anger to be anger?**

My therapist now assures me I've been
holding in my anger all these years,
but when I was a girl I didn't know
it was anger, or know I was holding it in.
I just knew I couldn't *do* anything about it
without making it worse, so I hid
as often as I could, for as long as I could.
In the basement, in closets. Hours at a time.
Just sat in the dark. He was my father.
I was told plenty often I *couldn't* be angry.
Who was there to tell me I could?

**Are victims of the actions of the angry the only victims of anger?
What about the angry themselves?**

Guy I knew once, Mack Eppson.  Nice guy,
used to play football, but wasn't very good.
Probably a little bigger than most others
at that point in junior high when they make you
the left guard, but didn't keep on growing,
so he just turned out a little husky
and a lot slow.  Went to a church college,
married a nice girl (they married in college,
they *were* still boy and girl), had two daughters
while his church back home put him through seminary.
They went to Djibouti as missionaries.
In a certain way of seeing things, a perfect life.
Anyway the life he insisted that he wanted.
But he hit them.  First his wife, Melinda.
(Everyone at their college thought it was cute,
both of them with M names: Mack and Melinda,
Melinda and Mack.  Though truth be told
he'd just made up Mack back in junior high,
to sound tougher.  His real name was Darryl.)

It wasn't from drinking, the hitting,
because he didn't drink, or anyway
I never knew him to, but it wasn't
something he *decided on*, exactly, either.
Back where I come from, the euphemism
was to *fly into a rage*.  "Then Momma
just flew into a rage," someone would say.
"Who knows why."  Like a bird into a windowpane.
I imagine his hitting Melinda had started
back in seminary, but she didn't leave him then.
Not until they were in Djibouti,
after he'd started hitting their girls, too.
You can't be a missionary if you're divorced,
not in his church anyway, so he went back home,
got hired on at the same mom and pop store

where he had bagged groceries in high school,
though by the time he came back it was a Safeway.
He's a manager now. Hasn't seen his daughters
since they were in grade school, or seen Melinda
since she left him. Didn't contest the divorce.
The girls are out of college now, not girls
anymore. I don't imagine they mean to visit him.
His father passed on a few years back, so he lives
in his parents' house, takes care of his mother.
Sleeps in the same room he slept in growing up.
Nice guy, works hard, played a little football once,
tried to do right, things don't always work out.

**Have I *chosen* anger or been chosen by it?**

I am angry, angry, angry.  I have no cause for anger,
living as I do the best of all possible lives,
the life than which none happier can be conceived.
But if others — fuck 'em all — can be depressed
without cause, I can damn well be angry.


**Who's entitled to host anger, and entitled by what?**

I warnt him and warnt him, but he jes kepp on.

164

**We learned our distance from the sun by measuring angles.**
**How discern our proximity to anger?**

Old couple who lived next door made a surprise visit one day.
We chatted pretty often over the hedge or in the driveway,
but otherwise they kept to themselves. That evening, though,
the doorbell rang while we were watching tv. It was Lily
bringing Vlad over to try to help him register that he was here
in Topeka, not in Chicago, where they had lived decades before,
and that we were the nice young couple next door to them now,
not the old friends they'd played pinochle with before they had kids.
Vlad stood in our living room, leaning on his walker, and tears
dripped from his chin onto the carpet. He said he *knew*
he was confused, but he still couldn't get straight in his head
who we were or where he was or when this all was taking place.

*That*'s how I feel in my violent episodes. They always start
with pain, excruciating pain, in my belly or in my teeth,
so I *know* I'm about to explode, even though I can't prevent it.
Soon enough, something Cheryl says will set me off. I'll *know*
I'm taking it wrong, but I can't stop suspecting her
of cheating on me, and the anger just gathers to my fists.
I hit her and throw her against the wall and onto the furniture.
The episodes occur even when she's pregnant. They only last
a few minutes, but that's plenty of time to hurt her, plenty
of time to ruin everything. I *know* I shouldn't be violent,
but the anger takes over. It's just like the sobbing afterward.
I know crying doesn't compensate, but the sorrow takes over.

**In what history is anger erased by, rather than an eraser of, persons?**

His gentleness to me, a protectiveness
archaic in manner and in measure,
was difficult to reconcile with his "list,"
the long, deeply ordinary catalog
of objects of his hatred: Catholics,
Jews, blacks, Mexicans. At other times, age,
alcohol, and idleness rendered him listless,
hazy. If I entered the living room,
where he sat alone all day behind closed blinds,
he would tell stories, as if to me, but really
to himself. Always the same few stories,
about the pitch-black dog he had as a boy.
Idly fingering, throughout the mumbled tales,
the small black ceramic dog statuette
that he kept on the table beside his chair.
Telling those stories, he hardly moved,
could hardly be heard. Launched into his list, though,
provoked by who knows what in his head,
his face turned red, his voice became abrasive,
his eyes blazed with a furious blindness.
At these moments there was no reaching him.
No touch, no gentle voice, could call him back.
Even so, only then, only when spitting
the list of those he hated, did he *move*,
gesturing, revived, enlivened by his rage.

**What is it to be *overcome* with anger?**

I was in the third grade when my father took me
to a baseball game, the minor-league team
a town or two down the road. A big deal
for us both: that's not the kind of Dad he was.
By the fifth inning, I was floating in soda
and had to pee. Off we went to the men's room.
I hadn't been in a stadium before,

I had to go, I didn't know all those men
were in line for the urinals, so I walked past.
The man at the front of the line (white shirt,
wool slacks and jacket, nice tie) tapped my shoulder.
"The line starts back there," he said, motioning
with his head, smiling, benign. Amused, I'm sure.
My father had fallen a few steps behind
when he'd paused to light up, so he arrived
just in time to see the short interaction.
I knew exactly what would happen next.
My father took a long draw on his cigarette,
then threw it at the wall with a flourish.
His words, loud enough to make sure everyone
was looking at him, came out as smoke. "Don't you
fuckin ever fuckin touch my fuckin son,"
he warned the man in the tie, whose eyes grew wide.
The man's smile went away. He looked confused.
My father pushed me to the side, not seeming
to notice how roughly, and then shoved the man,
his open palms butting against the man's chest.
The man, stumbling backward, arms flailing for balance,
was kept from falling by the concrete-block wall.
My Dad kept up. "Show him the goddam line
if you want, but keep your goddam office-soft
goddam slide-rule-using hands to your goddam self."
The man's leather-soled wing-tips were slick against
the cement floor; he kept pedaling for balance,
as if he were on ice and new to skates.
"I didn't…," he started to say, but stopped,
not sure how to finish the sentence he'd started.
As if my father gave him any time to.
He started punching at the man's face and head.
In my memory, there is a kind of symmetry
to the man's awkward flailing for balance
and my father's awkward flailing as he punched.
The man tried to cover his face, and tried
to turn away, but fell, sliding down the wall
until he landed on his right hip and elbow.

The button that had held the man's jacket closed
popped off as he fell.  My father went down
onto his knees to keep punching and punching.
It seemed like a long, long time before a few
of the other men began to intervene,
saying "Hey, hey, hey…" as they pulled my father
off the fallen man.  I had started crying.
One of the men holding my Dad away
from the fallen man called out "Somebody
go get a cop." My Dad elbowed himself free,
grabbed me by the arm, and dragged me to the car,
fast enough that I had to run to keep
from falling down.  Someone called out "Hey, you!"
after us, but we made it to the car.
He loved that car, a 64 Riviera nailhead
he came by God knows how, all beat up outside,
but he made me butter the seats and dash
once a week, so it was clean when we pulled out
from the gravel parking lot, windows open.
I was still crying, but once we reached the road,
my father backhanded me.  "Stop your bawling."
He caught me on the nose, one knuckle just right
to make my nose bleed, one ring just right to cut
my upper lip.  "Men don't cry" — I knew well
that warnings might come under cover of fact —
"and men don't let themselves get pushed around."
We drove a while in silence broken only
by my sniffling and wiping blood from my nose
onto the sleeve of my jacket.  "Time you learn
to fight back." He didn't look at me to say that,
didn't look at me the rest of the way home,
never took his eyes off the road, not to push in
the cigarette lighter, not to replace it.

## About the Author

H. L. Hix teaches at a university whose mascot is the cowboy, and whose business school has adopted as its official creed "The Code of the West," a bullet-point homage to cowboy movies, in a state vast portions of which are American Indian reservations.

[This page intentionally forfeited to fundamentalism.]

## APPARATUS

This is not a work of fiction / nor yet of one man:

## Attributions

The book's epigraph comes from Leo Madow, *Anger*. I have made one alteration in it, changing Madow's "mankind" to "humankind."

The section epigraphs come from the following sources:

"Aggression Cues": Howard Kassinove and Denis G. Sukhodolsky, "Anger Disorders: Basic Science and Practice Issues."

"The Plural of *Hate Speech*": Lauren Berlant, *Cruel Optimism*.

"The Anger Construct": Daniel M. Blonigen and Robert F. Krueger, "Human Quantitative Genetics of Aggression."

"Twenty Love Songs and a Measure of Disdain": Pablo Neruda, "Cuerpo de mujer..."

"Abscessive": Laura (Riding) Jackson, *The Laura (Riding) Jackson Reader*.

"God's Bounty": Gilles Deleuze, *Difference and Repetition*.

"Erinyeneutics": Slavoj Žižek, *The Year of Dreaming Dangerously*.

"Lost Wax": Sara Ahmed, *The Promise of Happiness*.

"Apparatus": Ezra Pound, *Cantos*.

"Erinyeneutics" consists of translations, as follows (with speaker identified, where relevant):

Fire, Venom: Aeschylus, *Agamemnon* 438-54: Chorus.

Wounds, Recklessness: Aeschylus, *Eumenides* 490-507: Chorus.

Horse, Girl: Aeschylus, *Suppliants* 418-37: Chorus.

Crop, Harvest: Aeschylus, *The Persians* 818-31: The Ghost of Darius.

Shriek, Shiver: Aeschylus, *Libation Bearers* 32-41: Chorus.

Fruit, Blood: Aeschylus, *Seven Against Thebes* 686-94: Chorus, then Eteocles, then Chorus.

As Best, Until: Aeschylus, *Prometheus Bound* 373-76: Prometheus.

His Half, Your Half: Sophocles, *King Oedipus* 404-7: Chorus.

Ever, When: Sophocles, *Oedipus at Colonus* 408-11: Oedipus and Ismene in dialogue, Oedipus first.

Flood, Wave: Sophocles, *Antigone* 705-18: Haemon.

Hers, Yours: Sophocles, *Electra* 369-71: Chorus.

Except, No Matter: Sophocles, *Ajax* 1330-41: Agamemnon, then Odysseus.

Suspend, Rebut: Sophocles, *Women of Trachis* 1114-19, 1134: Hyllus.

Oaths, Inscription: Sophocles, *Philoctetes* 1316-35: Neoptolemus.

Into, Against: Euripides, *Medea* 520-21: Chorus.

Out Of, Away From: Euripides, *Hippolytus* 1142-50: Chorus.

Into, Onto: Euripides, *Heracles* 1083-88: Amphitryon, then Chorus.

Oracles, Dreams: Euripides, *Iphigenia in Tauris* 1253-69: Chorus.

Ships, Horses: Euripides, *Iphigenia at Aulis* 77-83: Agamemnon.

Plea, Claim: Euripides, *Phoenician Women* 1447-50: Polyneices.

Earthen, Olympian: Euripides, *The Bacchae* 537-55: Chorus.

True, Bent: Plato, *Definitions* 415e

And, And: Plato, *Philebus* 47e: Socrates and Protarchus in dialogue, Socrates first.

Spirit, Dog: Plato, *Republic* 440c: Socrates.

Banishment, Return: Thucydides, *The History of the Peloponnesian War* 8.53-54

Demagogues, Sycophants: Diodorus Siculus, *Bibliotheke* XI 87.5

Risk, Grief: Philostratus, *Heroikos* 48.19-22

Lashes, Luxury: Seneca, *On Anger* II.5

Everything, Nothing: Sallust, *The War Against Catiline* X, XII

Fog, Hunger: Montaigne, from "On Anger"

Blood, Grapes: Juan Valera, from *Pepita Jimenez*

Figures, Phrases: Fernando Díaz-Plaja, from *The Spaniard and the Seven Deadly Sins*


"God's Bounty, as the Image of Desire Implicit in Images of Terror" responds to photographs by Freddy Alborta, Peter Andrews, Margaret Bourke-White, Larry Burrows, Alfred Eisenstaedt, John Paul Filo, Jan Grarup, Philip Jones Griffiths, Carol Guzy, Gary Haynes, Lewis Hine, Faleh Kheiber, Jerry Lampen, Mary Ellen Mark, Peter Marlow, Dylan Martinez, Don McCullin, Susan Meiselas, Bertrand Meunier, James Nachtwey, Eli Reed, Damir Sagolj, Sebastiao Salgado, the U. S. Air Force, and Carey Womack.

# Acknowledgments

I am grateful to the editors of the following journals for ushering into the world portions of this work: *Bat City Review, Copper Nickel, New York Quarterly, Salt Hill, South Dakota Review.*

In two cases the portion published so exceeded the standard measure of "journal length" as to merit particular mention. I thank Robert Hedin and Michael Waters for their largesse in presenting as part of *Great River Review* all the Greek tragedy translations together. I am grateful to Minna Proctor, under whose inspired editorship each issue of *TLR* has been conceived with a unifying vision, for envisioning "Aggression Cues" as an element of *TLR*'s "Long" issue.

The two poets who gave to earlier versions of this work perspicacious readings that intensified and shaped it are also persons to whom I was already indebted on other grounds. Indebted differently to each, but deeply to both, beyond any possibility of repayment to either. Phil, without whom not. Kate, without whom naught.

# Declaration

In this threnody the author bewails the numberless casualties of American anger: named few and nameless many, historical and contemporary, dead souls in ghost dance with dead bodies. And by occasion laments, as ruined and ruinous, our corrupted ideals, our delusion of height.

# Disclaimer

In his introduction to *The Origin of Species*, Darwin describes that book, despite its heft, as but an *abstract* of a much more comprehensive book, an abstract to be substituted, in deference to the pressures of reality, for the larger work, completion of which, because of its insistent ideality, receded toward an indefinite horizon. After years of dismissing Darwin's remark as affectation, here I stand, making the same apology he made: this book, page count notwithstanding, substitutes for, is merely an abstract of, an indefinitely large book.

Darwin's couching his excuse in personal terms (completion of the whole book would take more years than I can expect my imperfect health to allot me) *was* an affectation, in place of the real reason: the hypothetical book for which *The Origin of Species* supplies the abstract could not, even in principle, be completed, because its subject, though not *identical* to nature, is *coextensive* with nature. The hypothetical work for which *American Anger* substitutes could never be completed, either, for an analogous reason: its subject, though neither exhaustive of nor identical with human history, yet is coextensive with it.

That its indefinite extension in principle necessitates in practice an abstract holds true for *American Anger* not only topically, but also structurally: the variety of its modes could be added to indefinitely, and the number of its instances multiplied. Put another way: where evidence is limited or scant or elusive, it is susceptible to being marshalled, subjected to my ends, as in a court case. (*If the glove doesn't fit, you must acquit.*) Where evidence is *un*limited, though, where there is more evidence than could possibly be gathered or relayed, where the evidence is there for all to see, the power relation is inverted: I do not marshal, but instead am marshalled by, the evidence.

For what may this my abstract hope, for what might *any* abstract hope, in such circumstances? Not that the large book be completed by the author of the abstract, but that it be realized in the minds of the abstract's readers, that, in other words, the abstract reveal *as* evidence the evidence all around us, including and especially the evidence we ourselves are.

# Works Cited

I list here sources on which I have drawn directly. That I have not cited them individually does not diminish my indebtedness to other works the influence of which has been less immediate.

Abanes, Richard. *American Militias*. InterVarsity Press, 1996.

Abbott, Brett. *Engaged Observers: Documentary Photography Since the Sixties*. J. Paul Getty Museum, 2010.

Abdennur, Alexander. *Camouflaged Aggression: The Hidden Threat to Individuals and Organizations*. Detselig Enterprises, Ltd., 2000.

Acker, James R. *Scottsboro and Its Legacy: The Cases that Challenged American Legal and Social Justice*. Praeger, 2008.

Ahmed, Sara. *The Promise of Happiness*. Duke Univ. Press, 2010.

Aho, James A. *The Politics of Righteousness: Idaho Christian Patriotism*. Univ. of Washington Press, 1990.

Allman, T. D. *Rogue State: America at War with the World*. Nation Books, 2004.

Ambrose, Stephen E. "Atrocities in Historical Perspective." In Anderson, David L., 107-20.

Anderson, David L., ed. *Facing My Lai: Moving Beyond the Massacre*. Univ. Press of Kansas, 1998.

Anderson, Kristin L., and Debra Umberson. "Gendering Violence: Masculinity and Power in Men's Accounts of Domestic Violence." In Cromwell, 168-86.

Anon. *The Blue Book of the John Birch Society*. Western Islands, 1961.

Anon. "Self-defense provision restored ("Wyoming needs such a 'castle doctrine' bill")." *The Billings Gazette*. As posted at: http://www.freerepublic.com/focus/f-news/1974895/posts. Accessed 28 Nov. 2011.

Anon. *The State of the World*. Thames & Hudson, 2006.

Anon. *World Press Photo 10*. Thames & Hudson, 2010.

Antizzo, Glenn J. *U.S. Military Intervention in the Post-Cold War Era: How to Win America's Wars in the Twenty-First Century*. Louisiana State Univ. Press, 2010.

Arjet, Robert. " 'Man to Man': Power and Male Relationships in the Gunplay Film." In Springwood, 125-37.

Armstrong, Elisabeth, and Vijay Prashad. "Bandung Women: Vietnam, Afghanistan, Iraq, and the Necessary Risks of Solidarity." In Riley and Inayatullah, 15-49.

Arriola, Elvia R. "Accountability for Murder in the *Maquiladoras*: Linking Corporate Indifference to Gender Violence at the U.S.-Mexico Border." In Gaspar de Alba and Guzmán. 25-61.

Averill, James R. *Anger and Aggression: An Essay on Emotion.* Springer-Verlag, 1982.

Bacevich, Andrew J. *The New American Militarism: How Americans Are Seduced by War.* Oxford Univ. Press, 2005.

Baiamonte, John V., Jr. *Spirit of Vengeance: Nativism and Louisiana Justice, 1921-1924.* Louisiana State Univ. Press, 1986.

Baird-Windle, Patricia, and Eleanor J. Bader. *Targets of Hatred: Anti-Abortion Terrorism.* Palgrave, 2001.

Baldwin, James. *The Evidence of Things Not Seen.* Holt, Rinehart and Winston, 1985.

Barash, David P. *Beloved Enemies: Our Need for Opponents.* Prometheus Books, 1994.

Barkun, Michael. *Religion and the Racist Right: The Origins of the Christian Identity Movement.* Rev. Ed. Univ. of North Carolina Press, 1997.

Barlow, Hugh D., and David Kauzlarich. *Explaining Crime: A Primer in Criminological Theory.* Rowman & Littlefield, 2010.

Barnet, Richard J. *The Economy of Death.* Atheneum, 1969.

Beck, Aaron T. *Prisoners of Hate: The Cognitive Basis of Anger, Hostility, and Violence.* HarperCollins, 1999.

Bell, Jeannine. *Policing Hatred: Law Enforcement, Civil Rights, and Hate Crime.* New York Univ. Press, 2002.

Bellamy, Alex J. *Fighting Terror: Ethical Dilemmas.* Zed Books, 2008.

Bellesiles, Michael A. *Arming America: The Origins of a National Gun Culture.* Alfred A. Knopf, 2000.

Belohlavek, John. "Race, Progress, and Destiny: Caleb Cushing and the Quest for American Empire." In Haynes and Morris, 21-47.

Benedek, Thomas. "The 'Tuskegee Study' of Syphilis: Analysis of Moral versus Methodologic Aspects." In Reverby, *Tuskegee's Truths,* 213-35.

Berman, Daniel M. *Death on the Job: Occupational Health and Safety Struggles in the United States.* Monthly Review Press, 1978.

Bierman, Harold, Jr. *Accounting/Finance Lessons of Enron: A Case Study.* World Scientific, 2008.

Bilton, Michael, and Kevin Sim. *Four Hours in My Lai.* Viking, 1992.

Blanchard, D. Caroline, and Robert J. Blanchard. "Stress and Aggressive Behaviors." In Nelson, *Biology of Aggression.* 275-91.

Blanchard, Dallas A., and Terry J. Prewitt. *Religious Violence and Abortion: The Gideon Project.* Univ. Press of Florida, 1993.

Blue, Ethan. "The Strange Career: Remaking Manhood and Medicine at San Quentin State Penitentiary, 1913-1951." *Pacific Historical Review* 78:2 (May 2009): 210-41.

Blumberg, Paul. *The Predatory Society: Deception in the American Marketplace.* Oxford Univ. Press, 1989.

Bogard, William. *The Bhopal Tragedy: Language, Logic,, and Politics in the Production of a Hazard.* Westview Press, 1989.

Boggs, Carl. *The Crimes of Empire: Rogue Superpower and World Domination.* Pluto Press, 2010.

Brandt, Allan M. "Racism and Research: The Case of the Tuskegee Syphilis Experiment." In Reverby, *Tuskegee's Truths,* 15-33.

Bratich, Jack Z. *Conspiracy Panics: Political Rationality and Popular Culture.* SUNY Press, 2008.

Briggs, Jean L. *Never in Anger: Portrait of an Eskimo Family.* Harvard Univ. Press, 1970.

Brownridge, Douglas A. *Violence Against Women: Vulnerable Populations.* Routledge, 2009.

Broyles, John Allen. *The John Birch Society as a Movement of Social Protest of the Radical Right.* Ph.D. dissertation, Boston University, 1963.

Bruneau, Thomas C. *Patriots for Profit: Contractors and the Military in U.S. National Security.* Stanford Univ. Press, 2011.

Bryce, Robert. *Pipe Dreams: Greed, Ego, and the Death of Enron.* PublicAffairs, 2002.

Buchheit, Paul, ed. *American Wars: Illusions and Realities.* Clarity Press, 2008.

Buley, Benjamin. *The New American Way of War: Military Culture and the Political Utility of Force.* Routledge, 2008.

Burns, John W., et al. "Anger Inhibition and Pain: Conceptualizations, Evidence and New Directions." *Journal of Behavioral Medicine* 31 (2008): 259-79.

Burr, George Lincoln, ed. *Narratives of the Witchcraft Cases 1648-1706.* Charles Scribner's Sons, 1914.

Burton, Jeffery F., et al. *Confinement and Ethnicity: An Overview of World War II Japanese American Relocation Sites.* Univ. of Washington Press, 2002.

Buxton, Peter. "Testimony by Peter Buxton from the United States Hearings on Human Experimentation, 1973." In Reverby, *Tuskegee's Truths,* 150-56.

Carter, Dan T. *Scottsboro: A Tragedy of the American South.* Revised Ed. Louisiana St. Univ. Press, 1979.

Chalmers, David M. *Hooded Americanism: The First Century of the Ku Klux Klan.* Doubleday, 1965.

Chang, Gordon H., ed. *Morning Glory, Evening Shadow: Yamato Ichihashi and His Internment Writings, 1942-1945.* Stanford Univ. Press, 1997.

Chasin, Barbara H. *Inequality and Violence in the United States: Casualties of Capitalism.* Humanities Press, 1997.

Chishti, Anees. *Dateline Bhopal: A Newsman's Diary of the Gas Disaster.* Concept Publishing, 1986.

Churchill, Robert H. *To Shake Their Guns in the Tyrant's Face: Libertarian Political Violence and the Origins of the Militia Movement.* Univ. of Michigan Press, 2009.

Clapp, Jennifer. *Toxic Exports: The Transfer of Hazardous Wastes from Rich to Poor Countries.* Cornell Univ. Press, 2001.

Clinton, William J. "Statement On The Korean War No Gun Ri Incident." *Weekly Compilation Of Presidential Documents* 37.2 (2001): 88.

Coffin, Morse H. *The Battle of Sand Creek.* Ed. Alan W. Farley. W. M. Morrison, 1965.

Cohen, Don, and Angela K.-y. Leung. "Violence and Character: A CuPS (Culture x Person x Situation) Perspective." In Shaver and Mikulincer, 187-200.

Comstock, Gary David. *Violence Against Lesbians and Gay Men.* Columbia Univ. Press, 1991.

Córdoba, María Socorro Tabuenca. "Ghost Dance in Ciudad Juárez at the End/Beginning of the Millennium." Ed. and trans. Georgina Guzmán. In Gaspar de Alba and Guzmán. 95-119.

Corn, Jacqueline. "Protective Legislation for Coal Miners, 1870-1900: Response to Safety and Health Hazards." In Rosner and Markowitz. 67-82.

Cortner, Richard C. *A Mob Intent on Death: The NAACP and the Arkansas Riot Cases.* Wesleyan Univ. Press, 1988.

Cramer, Clayton E. *Armed America: The Remarkable Story of How and Why Guns Became as American as Apple Pie.* Nelson Current, 2006.

Cromwell, Paul, ed. *In Their Own Words: Criminals on Crime: an Anthology.* Fifth Ed. Oxford Univ. Press, 2010.

Crothers, Lane. *Rage on the Right: The American Militia Movement from Ruby Ridge to Homeland Security.* Rowman & Littlefield, 2003.

Cruver, Brian. *Anatomy of Greed: The Unshredded Truth from an Enron Insider.* Carroll & Graf, 2002.

Cullen, Dave. *Columbine.* Twelve, 2009.

Dali, Salvador. "The Stinking Ass." In *Art in Theory 1900-2000: An Anthology of Changing Ideas*. Ed. Charles Harrison and Paul J. Wood. 2nd Ed. Wiley-Blackwell, 2002. 486-89.

Das Gupta, Monisha. "Bewildered? Women's Studies and the War on Terror." In Riley and Inayatullah, 129-53.

Davis, David Brion, ed. *The Fear of Conspiracy: Images of Un-American Subversion from the Revolution to the Present*. Cornell Univ. Press, 1971.

DeJong, William, Joel C. Epstein, and Thomas E. Hart. "Bad Things Happen in Good Communities: The Rampage Shooting in Edinboro, Pennsylvania, and Its Aftermath." In Moore, Mark H., et al., eds. *Deadly Lessons: Understanding Lethal School Violence*. The National Academies Press, 2002. 70-100.

DeKeseredy, Walter S. *Violence Against Women: Myths, Facts, Controversies*. Univ. of Toronto Press, 2011.

Denham, Gayle, and Kaye Bultemeier. "Anger: Targets and Triggers." In Thomas, *Women and Anger*. 68-90.

DeWall, C. Nathan, and Craig A. Anderson. "The General Aggression Model." In Shaver and Mikulincer. 15-33.

DiGiuseppe, Raymond, and Raymond Chip Tafrate. *Understanding Anger Disorders*. Oxford Univ. Press, 2007.

Dobrin, Adam, Brian Wiersema, Colin Loftin, and David McDowall, eds. *Statistical Handbook of Violence in America*. Oryx Press, 1996.

Dodge, Kenneth A. "Social Information Processing Patterns as Mediators of the Interaction Between Genetic Factors and Life Experiences in the Development of Aggressive Behavior." In Shaver and Mikulincer. 165-85.

Durham, Martin. *White Rage: The Extreme Right and American Politics*. Routledge, 2007.

Dusselier, Jane E. *Artifacts of Loss: Crafting Survival in Japanes American Concentration Camps*. Rutgers Univ. Press, 2008.

Dutton, Donald G. "Attachment and Violence: An Anger Born of Fear." In Shaver and Mikulincer, 259-75.

Dyer, Joel. *Harvest of Rage: Why Oklahoma City Is Only the Beginning*. Westview Press, 1997.

Eckhardt, William G., Ron Ridenhour, and Hugh C. Thompson, Jr. "Experiencing the Darkness: An Oral History." In Anderson, David L., 27-51.

Ehrenreich, Barbara. *Blood Rites: Origins and History of the Passions of War*. Metropolitan Books, 1997.

Ehrlich, Howard J. *Hate Crimes and Ethnoviolence: The History, Current Affairs, and Future of Discrimination in America.* Westview Press, 2009.

Ellis, John. *The Social History of the Machine Gun.* Pantheon Books, 1975.

Epstein, Benjamin R., and Arnold Foster. *Report on the John Birch Society 1966.* Random House, 1966.

Farber, I. E., Harry F. Harlow, and Louis Jolyon West. "Brainwashing, Conditioning, and DDD (Debility, Dependency, and Dread)." *Sociometry* 20:4 (December 1957): 271-85.

Faux, Marian. *Crusaders: Voices from the Abortion Front.* Birch Lane Press, 1990.

Feagin, Joe R. *Systematic Racism: A Theory of Oppression.* Routledge, 2006.

Feld, Steven. *Sound and Sentiment: Birds, Weeping, Poetics, and Song in Kaluli Expression.* Univ. of Pennsylvania Press, 1982.

Finch, Phillip. *God, Guts, and Guns.* Seaview/Putnam, 1983.

Fleisher, Kass. *The Bear River Massacre and the Making of History.* SUNY Press, 2004.

Fletcher, Thomas H. *From Love Canal to Environmental Justice: The Politics of Hazardous Waste on the Canada-U.S. Border.* Broadview Press, 2003.

Fogarty, Robert S. "An Age of Wisdom, An Age of Foolishness: The Davidians, Some Forerunners, and Our Age." In Wright, Stuart A. 3-19.

Ford, Franklin L. *Political Murder: From Tyrannicide to Terrorism.* Harvard Univ. Press, 1985.

Fox, Loren. *Enron: The Rise and Fall.* John Wiley & Sons, 2003.

Frey, Robert Seitz, and Nancy Thompson-Frey. *The Silent and the Damned: The Murder of Mary Phagan and the Lynching of Leo Frank.* Madison Books, 1988.

Fried, Albert, ed. *McCarthyism: The Great American Red Scare.* Oxford Univ. Press, 1997.

Fried, Richard M. *Nightmare in Red: The McCarthy Era in Perspective.* Oxford Univ. Press, 1990.

Frost, Natasha A. *The Punitive State: Crime, Punishment, and Imprisonment across the United States.* LFB Scholarly Publishing LLC, 2006.

Fuentes, Annette. *Lockdown High: When the Schoolhouse Becomes a Jailhouse.* Verso, 2011.

Gaspar de Alba, Alicia, ed., with Georgina Guzmán. *Making a Killing: Femicide, Free Trade, and* La Frontera. Univ. of Texas Press, 2010.

Gaspar de Alba, Alicia. "Poor Brown Female: The Miller's Compensation for 'Free' Trade." In Gaspar de Alba and Guzmán. 63-93.

Gaylin, Willard. *The Rage Within: Anger in Modern Life.* Simon and Schuster,

1984.

Gersuny, Carl. *Work Hazards and Industrial Conflict.* Univ. Press of New England, 1981.

Gibbs, Lois Marie. *Love Canal: My Story.* With Murray Levine. SUNY Press, 1982.

Gibson, James William. *Warrior Dreams: Paramilitary Culture in Post-Vietnam America.* Hill and Wang, 1994.

Gilligan, James. *Violence: Our Deadly Epidemic and Its Causes.* G. P. Putnam's Sons, 1996.

Giroux, Henry A. *Beyond the Spectacle of Terrorism: Global Uncertainty and the Challenge of the New Media.* Paradigm Publishers, 2006.

Gitlin, Martin. *The Ku Klux Klan: A Guide to an American Subculture.* Greenwood Press, 2009.

Glick, Robert A., and Steven P. Roose, eds. *Rage, Power, and Aggression.* Yale Univ. Press, 1993.

Go, Julian. *Patterns of Empire: The British and American Empires, 1688 to the Present.* Cambridge Univ. Press, 2011.

Golden, Harry. *A Little Girl Is Dead.* World Publishing, 1965.

Golden, Reuel. *Photojournalism 1855 to the Present: Editor's Choice.* Abbeville Press, 2005.

Goldstein, Arnold P. *Violence in America: Lessons on Understanding the Aggression in Our Lives.* Davies-Black Publishing, 1996.

Goodman, James. *Stories of Scottsboro.* Pantheon Books, 1994.

Gorfinkel, Claire, ed. *The Evacuation Diary of Hatsuye Egami.* Intentional Productions, 1995.

Graebner, William. "Hegemony Through Science: Information Engineering and Lead Toxicology." In Rosner and Markowitz. 140-59.

Grant, Nicole J. *The Selling of Contraception: The Dalkon Shield Case, Sexuality, and Women's Autonomy.* Ohio State Univ. Press, 1992.

Greene, Judith A. "Entrepreneurial Corrections: Incarceration As a Business Opportunity." In Mauer and Chesney-Lind, 95-113.

Griffin, Susan. *A Chorus of Stones: The Private Life of War.* Doubleday, 1992.

Griffith, Robert. *The Politics of Fear: Joseph R. McCarthy and the Senate.* Second ed. Univ. of Massachusetts Press, 1987.

Grossman, Arnold. *One Nation Under Guns: An Essay on an American Epidemic.* Fulcrum Publishing, 2006.

Grossman, Dave. *On Killing: The Psychological Cost of Learning to Kill in War and Society.* Little, Brown, 1995.

Grove, Gene. *Inside the John Birch Society.* Gold Medal Books, 1961.

Guiora, Amos N. *Constitutional Limits on Coercive Interrogation.* Oxford Univ. Press, 2008.

Gutstein, Donald. *Not a Conspiracy Theory: How Business Propaganda Hijacks Democracy.* Key Porter Books, 2009.

Hall, John R. "Public Narratives and the Apocalyptic Sect: From Jonestown to Mt. Carmel." In Wright, Stuart A. 205-35.

Halperin, Eran. "The Emotional Roots of Intergroup Aggression: The Distinct Roles of Anger and Hatred." In Shaver and Mikulincer. 315-31.

Hanley, Charles J. "No Gun Ri." *Critical Asian Studies* 42.4 (2010): 589-622.

Hayashi, Brian Masaru. *Democratizing the Enemy: the Japanese American Internment.* Princeton Univ. Press, 2004.

Haynes, Gary. *Picture This!: The Inside Story and Classic Photos of UPI Newspictures.* Bulfinch Press, 2006.

Haynes, Sam W., and Christopher Morris, eds. *Manifest Destiny and Empire: American Antebellum Expansionism.* Texas A&M Univ. Press, 1997.

Heale, M. J. *McCarthy's Americans: Red Scare Politics in State and Nation, 1935-1965.* Univ. of Georgia Press, 1998.

Hedges, Chris. *American Fascists: The Christian Right and the War on America.* Free Press, 2007.

Heifetz, Ruth. "Women, Lead, and Reproductive Hazards: Defining a New Risk." In Rosner and Markowitz. 160-73.

Hejdenberg, Jennie, and Bernice Andrews. "The Relationship Between Shame and Different Types of Anger." *Personality and Individual Differences* 50:8 (June 2011): 1278-82.

Herbert, T. Walter. *Sexual Violence and American Manhood.* Harvard Univ. Press, 2002.

Hernan, Robert Emmet. *This Borrowed Earth: Lessons from the 15 Worst Environmental Disasters Around the World.* Palgrave Macmillan, 2010.

Herring, George C. "What Kind of War Was the Vietnam War?" In Anderson, David L., 95-105.

Hietala, Thomas R. "'This Splendid Juggernaut': Westward a Nation and Its People." In Haynes and Morris, 48-67.

Hirabayashi, Lane Ryo, with Kenichiro Shimada. *Japanese American Resettlement Through the Lens: Hikaru Carl Iwasaki and the WRA's Photographic Section, 1943-1945.* Univ. Press of Colorado, 2009.

Hofstadter, Richard. *The Paranoid Style in American Politics and Other Essays.* Harvard Univ. Press, 1996.

Hoig, Stan. *The Sand Creek Massacre.* Univ. of Oklahoma Press, 1961.

Honigsberg, Peter Jan. *Our Nation Unhinged: The Human Consequences of the War on Terror.* Univ. of California Press, 2009.

Hornblum, Allen M. *Acres of Skin: Human Experiments at Holmesburg Prison.* Routledge, 1998.

----------. *Sentenced to Science: One Black Man's Story of Imprisonment in America.* Penn State Univ. Press, 2007.

Horsman, Reginald. *Race and Manifest Destiny: The Origins of American Racial Anglo-Saxonism.* Harvard Univ. Press, 1981.

Howard, John. *Concentration Camps on the Home Front: Japanese Americans in the House of Jim Crow.* Univ. of Chicago Press, 2008.

Ishizuka, Karen L. *Lost and Found: Reclaiming the Japanese American Incarceration.* Univ. of Illinois Press, 2006.

Johannsen, Robert W. "The Meaning of Manifest Destiny." In Haynes and Morris, 7-20.

Johnson, Chalmers. *Blowback: The Costs and Consequences of American Empire.* Metropolitan Books, 2000.

Johnson, George. *Architects of Fear: Conspiracy Theories and Paranoia in American Politics.* Jeremy P. Tarcher, Inc., 1983.

Johnson, Haynes. *The Age of Anxiety: McCarthyism to Terrorism.* Harcourt, 2005.

Jones, James H. *Bad Blood: The Tuskegee Syphilis Experiment.* New and Expanded Edition. The Free Press, 1993.

Jones, Tara. *Corporate Killing: Bhopals Will Happen.* Free Association Books, 1988.

Kappeler, Susanne. *The Will to Violence: The Politics of Personal Behaviour.* Teachers College Press, 1995.

Kassinove, Howard, ed. *Anger Disorders: Definition, Diagnosis, and Treatment.* Taylor & Francis, 1995.

----------, and Denis G. Sukhodolsky. "Anger Disorders: Basic Science and Practice Issues." In Kassinove, 1-26.

Kastor, Peter J. *America's Struggle with Empire: A Documentary History.* CQ Press, 2010.

Kellner, Douglas. *Guys and Guns Amok: Domestic Terrorism and School Shootings from the Oklahoma City Bombing to the Virginia Tech Massacre.* Paradigm Publishers, 2008.

Kelly, Tobias. *This Side of Silence: Human Rights, Torture, and the Recognition of Cruelty.* Univ. of Pennsylvania Press, 2012.

185

King, C. Richard. "Arming Desire: The Sexual Force of Guns in the United States." In Springwood, 87-97.

Klama, John. *Aggression: The Myth of the Beast Within.* John Wiley & Sons, 1988.

Klare, Michael T. *Resource Wars: The New Landscape of Global Conflict.* Metropolitan Books, 2001.

Klein, Renate. *Responding to Intimate Violence Against Women: The Role of Informal Networks.* Cambridge Univ. Press, 2012.

Kochi, Tarik. *The Other's War: Recognition and the Violence of Ethics.* Birkbeck Law Press, 2009.

Kohn, Abigail A. *Shooters: Myths and Realities of America's Gun Cultures.* Oxford Univ. Press, 2004.

Konner, Melvin J. "Do We Need Enemies?: The Origins and Consequences of Rage." In Glick and Roose, 173-93.

Kreienbrock, Jörg. *Malicious Objects, Anger Management, and the Question of Modern Literature.* Fordham Univ. Press, 2013.

Kurzman, Dan. *A Killing Wind: Inside Union Carbide and the Bhopal Catastrophe.* McGraw-Hill, 1987.

Lacayo, Richard, and George Russell. *Eyewitness: 150 Years of Photojournalism.* Oxmoor House, Inc., 1990.

Laqueur, Walter. *No End to War: Terrorism in the Twenty-First Century.* Continuum, 2003.

Larkin, Ralph W. *Comprehending Columbine.* Temple Univ. Press, 2007.

Lawrence, Frederick M. *Punishing Hate: Bias Crimes under American Law.* Harvard Univ. Press, 1999.

Lawson, Gary, and Guy Seidman. *The Constitution of Empire: Territorial Expansion and American Legal History.* Yale Univ. Press, 2004.

Lazreg, Marnia. *Torture and the Twilight of Empire: From Algiers to Baghdad.* Princeton Univ. Press, 2007.

Legault, Richard L. *Trends in American Gun Ownership.* LFB Scholarly Publishing LLC, 2008.

Lens, Sidney. *Permanent War: The Militarization of America.* Schocken Books, 1987.

Levine, Adeline Gordon. *Love Canal: Science, Politics, and People.* Lexington Books, 1982.

Linfield, Susie. *The Cruel Radiance: Photography and Political Violence.* Univ. of Chicago Press, 2010.

Lorenz, Konrad. *On Aggression.* Trans. Marjorie Kerr Wilson. Harcourt, Brace

& World, 1966.

McCullough, Michael E., Robert Kurzban, and Benjamin A. Tabak. "Evolved Mechanisms for Revenge and Forgiveness." In Shaver and Mikulincer, 221-39.

McGlashan, Colin. As cited in Toch, Preface to *Violent Men*.

McMillen, Persis W. *Currents of Malice: Mary Towne Esty and Her Family in Salem Witchcraft*. Peter E. Randall Publisher, 1990.

Madow, Leo. *Anger*. Charles Scribner's Sons, 1972.

Mahapatra, Chintamani. *The US Approach to the Islamic World in Post-9/11 Era: Implications for India*. Academic Foundation, 2009.

Manuck, Stephen B., Jay R. Kaplan, and Francis E. Lotrich. "Brain Serotonin and Aggressive Disposition in Humans and Nonhuman Primates." In Nelson, *Biology of Aggression*. 65-113.

Mark, Vernon H., and Frank R. Ervin. *Violence and the Brain*. Harper & Row, 1970.

Marsden, George M. *Fundamentalism and American Culture*. Second Edition. Oxford Univ. Press, 2006.

Mather, Cotton. *On Witchcraft*. The Peter Pauper Press, no date.

Matza, David. *Becoming Deviant*. Prentice-Hall, 1969.

Mauer, Marc, and Meda Chesney-Lind, eds. *Invisible Punishment: The Collateral Consequences of Mass Imprisonment*. The New Press, 2002.

Mayer, Jane. "Outsourcing Torture: The Secret History of America's 'Extraordinary Rendition' Program." In *The United States and Torture: Interrogations, Incarceration, and Abuse*. Ed. Marjorie Cohn. New York Univ. Press, 2011. 137-60.

Messner, Steven F., and Richard Rosenfeld. *Crime and the American Dream*. Fourth Ed. Thomson Wadsworth, 2007.

Miller, James A. *Remembering Scottsboro: The Legacy of an Infamous Trial*. Princeton Univ. Press, 2009.

Miller, Rod. *Massacre at Bear River: First, Worst, Forgotten*. Caxton Press, 2008.

Mintz, Morton. *At Any Cost: Corporate Greed, Women, and the Dalkon Shield*. Pantheon Books, 1985.

Mokhiber, Russell. *Corporate Crime and Violence: Big Business Power and the Abuse of the Public Trust*. Sierra Club Books, 1988.

Moyer, K. E. *The Physiology of Hostility*. Markham Publishing Co., 1971.

Muppidi, Himadeep. "Shame and Rage: International Relations and the World School of Colonialism." In Riley and Inayattulah, 51-61.

Myers, Gustavus. *History of Bigotry in the United States*. Ed. Henry R.

Christman. Capricorn Books, 1960.

National Research Council. *Firearms and Violence: A Critical Review.* Charles F. Wellford, John V. Pepper, and Carol V. Petrie, eds. Committee on Law and Justice, Division of Behavioral and Social Sciences and Education. The National Academies Press, 2005.

Neiwert, David A. *In God's Country: The Patriot Movement and the Pacific Northwest.* WSU Press, 1999.

Nelkin, Dorothy, and Michael S. Brown. *Workers at Risk: Voices from the Workplace.* Univ. of Chicago Press, 1984.

Nelson, Randy J., ed. *Biology of Aggression.* Oxford Univ. Press, 2006.

Nesbitt, Richard E., and Dov Cohen. *Culture of Honor: The Psychology of Violence in the American South.* Westview Press, 1996.

Newport, Kenneth G. C. *The Branch Davidians of Waco: The History and Beliefs of an Apocalyptic Sect.* Oxford Univ. Press, 2006.

Newton, Michael. *The Ku Klux Klan: History, Organization, Language, Influence and Activities of America's Most Notorious Secret Society.* McFarland & Co., 2007.

Nguyen, Tram. *We Are All Suspects Now: Untold Stories from Immigrant Communities after 9/11.* Beacon Press, 2005.

Nugent, Walter. *Habits of Empire: A History of American Expansion.* Alfred A. Knopf, 2008.

Nussbaum, Martha C. *Hiding from Humanity: Disgust, Shame, and the Law.* Princeton Univ. Press, 2004.

Oliver, Kendrick. *The My Lai Massacre in American History and Memory.* Manchester Univ. Press, 2006.

Olson, James S., and Randy Roberts. *My Lai: A Brief History with Documents.* Bedford Books, 1998.

Otterman, Michael. *American Torture: From the Cold War to Abu Ghraib and Beyond.* Pluto Press, 2007.

Ovsiew, Fred, and Stuart Yudofsky. "Aggression: A Neuropsychiatric Perspective." In Glick and Roose, 213-30.

Paglen, Trevor, and A. C. Thompson. *Torture Taxi: On the Trail of the CIA's Rendition Flights.* Melville House Publishing, 2006.

Parenti, Michael. *The Face of Imperialism.* Paradigm Publishers, 2011.

----------. *To Kill a Nation: The Attack on Yugoslavia.* Verso, 2000.

Parker, Howard J. *View from the Boys: A Sociology of Down-Town Adolescents.* David & Charles, 1974.

Peek, Lori. *Behind the Backlash: Muslim Americans after 9/11.* Temple Univ.

Press, 2011.

Peers, Lt. Gen. W. R. *The My Lai Inquiry*. W. W. Norton, 1979.

Perry, Susan, and Jim Dawson. *Nightmare: Women and the Dalkon Shield*. Macmillan, 1985.

Person, Ethel Spector. "Male Sexuality and Power." In Glick and Roose, 29-44.

Pfaff, William. *The Irony of Manifest Destiny: The Tragedy of America's Foreign Policy*. Walker & Co., 2010.

Phillips, Joshua E. S. *None of Us Were Like This Before: American Soldiers and Torture*. Verso, 2010.

Pogrebin, Mark R., et al. "Retrospective Accounts of Violent Events by Gun Offenders." In Cromwell, 187-201.

Quarles, Chester L. *The Ku Klux Klan and Related American Racialist and Antisemitic Organizations: A History and Analysis*. McFarland & Co., 1999.

Reavis, Dick J. *The Ashes of Waco: An Investigation*. Simon & Schuster, 1995.

Rees, John. *Imperialism and Resistance*. Routledge, 2006.

Reverby, Susan M. *Examining Tuskegee: The Infamous Syphilis Study and Its Legacy*. Univ. of North Carolina Press, 2009.

----------, ed. *Tuskegee's Truths: Rethinking the Tuskegee Syphilis Study*. Univ. of North Carolina Press, 2000.

Ribuffo, Leo P. *The Old Christian Right: The Protestant Far Right from the Great Depression to the Cold War*. Temple Univ. Press, 1983.

Rice, Condoleezza. "Rethinking the National Interest." *Foreign Affairs* 87:4 (July/August 2008): 2-26.

Richie, Beth E. "The Social Impact of Mass Incarceration on Women." In Mauer and Chesney-Lind, 136-49.

Riley, Robin L., and Naeem Inayatullah, eds. *Interrogating Imperialism: Conversations on Gender, Race, War*. Palgrave Macmillan, 2006.

Risen, James, and Judy L. Thomas. *Wrath of Angels: The American Abortion War*. Basic Books, 1998.

Robbins, Thomas, and Dick Anthony. "Sects and Violence: Factors Enhancing the Volatility of Marginal Religious Movements." In Wright, Stuart A. 236-59.

Robins, Robert S., and Jerrold M. Post. *Political Paranoia: The Psychopolitics of Hatred*. Yale Univ. Press, 1997.

Romito, Patrizia. *A Deafening Silence: Hidden Violence Against Women and Children*. Trans. Janet Eastwood. The Policy Press, 2008.

Rosner, David, and Gerald Markowitz, eds. *Dying for Work: Workers' Safety and Health in Twentieth-Century America*. Indiana Univ. Press, 1987.

Rosner, David, and Gerald Markowitz. " 'A Gift of God'?: The Public Health Controversy over Leaded Gasoline during the 1920s." In Rosner and Markowitz. 121-39.

Russell, Sheryl S., and Barbara Shirk. "Women's Anger and Eating." In Thomas, *Women and Anger*. 170-85.

Ryan, William. *Blaming the Victim*. Pantheon Books, 1971.

Salinger, Kurt. "A Behavior-Analytic View of Anger and Aggression." In Kassinove, 69-79.

Salter, Malcolm S. *Innovation Corrupted: The Origins and Legacy of Enron's Collapse*. Harvard Univ. Press, 2008.

Sargent, Lyman Tower, ed. *Extremism in America: A Reader*. New York Univ. Press, 1995.

Savitt, Todd L. "The Use of Blacks for Medical Experimentation and Demonstration in the Old South." *Journal of Southern History* 48:3 (1982): 331-48.

Scheff, Thomas J. *Bloody Revenge: Emotions, Nationalism, and War*. Westview Press, 1994.

Sell, Aaron. "Applying Adaptationism to Human Anger: The Recalibrational Theory." In Shaver and Mikulincer. 53-70.

Shalom, Stephen Rosskamm. *Imperial Alibis: Rationalizing U.S. Intervention After the Cold War*. South End Press, 1993.

Shaver, Phillip R., and Mario Mikulincer, eds. *Human Aggression and Violence: Causes, Manifestations, and Consequences*. American Psychological Association, 2011.

Shaver, Phillip R., Michal Segev, and Mario Mikulincer. "A Behavioral Systems Perspective on Power and Aggression." In Shaver and Mikulincer. 71-87.

Shiekh, Irum. *Detained without Cause: Muslims' Stories of Detention and Deportation in America after 9/11*. Palgrave Macmillan, 2011.

Shogan, Robert. *No Sense of Decency: The Army-McCarthy Hearings: A Demagogue Falls and Television Takes Charge of American Politics*. Ivan R. Dee, 2009.

Shrivastava, Paul. *Bhopal: Anatomy of a Crisis*. Ballinger Publishing Co., 1987.

Siann, Gerda. *Accounting for Aggression: Perspectives on Aggression and Violence*. Allen & Unwin, 1985.

Singular, Stephen. *The Wichita Divide: The Murder of Dr. George Tiller and the Battle over Abortion*. St. Martin's Press, 2011.

Skrapec, Candice. "'The Morgue Was Really from the Dark Ages': Insights from a Forensic Psychologist." In Gaspar de Alba and Guzmán. 245-53.

Slotter, Erica B., and Eli J. Finkel. "I³ Theory: Instigating, Impelling, and Inhibiting Factors in Aggression." In Shaver and Mikulincer. 35-52.

Spielberger, Charles D., Eric C. Reheiser, and Sumner J. Sydeman. "Measuring the Experience, Expression, and Control of Anger." In Kassinove, 49-67.

Springwood, Charles Fruehling, ed. *Open Fire: Understanding Global Gun Cultures*. Berg, 2007.

----------. "Gunscapes: Toward a Global Geography of the Firearm." In Springwood, 15-27.

Stanley, L. L. "An Analysis of One Thousand Testicular Substance Implantations." *Endocrinology* 6 (1922): 787-94.

State University of New York. *No Gun Ri Archives*. http://www.albany.edu/nogunrimemory/

Stearns, Carol Zisowitz, and Peter N. Stearns. *Anger: The Struggle for Emotional Control in America's History*. Univ. of Chicago Press, 1986.

Steinhauer, Jennifer. "Despite Tearful Pleas, No Real Chance." *The New York Times* 162:56,110 (18 April 2013): A1, A15.

Stern, Kenneth S. *A Force Upon the Plain: The American Militia Movement and the Politics of Hate*. Simon & Schuster, 1996.

Stock, Catherine McNicol. *Rural Radicals: Righteous Rage in the American Grain*. Cornell Univ. Press, 1996.

Stockley, Grif. *Blood in Their Eyes: The Elaine Race Massacres of 1919*. Univ. of Arkansas Press, 2001.

Strozier, Charles B. *Apocalypse: On the Psychology of Fundamentalism in America*. Beacon Press, 1994.

Sufrin, Sidney C. *Bhopal: Its Setting, Responsibility and Challenge*. Ajanta Publications, 1985.

Suhi, Choi. "Silencing Survivors' Narratives: Why Are We Again Forgetting The No Gun Ri Story?." *Rhetoric & Public Affairs* 11.3 (2008): 367-388.

Svaldi, David. *Sand Creek and the Rhetoric of Extermination: A Case Study in Indian-White Relations*. Univ. Press of America, 1989.

Szymanski, Albert. *The Logic of Imperialism*. Praeger, 1981.

Tabor, James D., and Eugene V. Gallagher. *Why Waco?: Cults and the Battle for Religious Freedom in America*. Univ. of California Press, 1995.

Tafrate, Raymond Chip. "Evaluation of Treatment Strategies for Adult Anger Disorders." In Kassinove, 109-29.

Thibodeau, David, and Leon Whiteson. *A Place Called Waco: A Survivor's Story*. Public Affairs, 1999.

Thomaes, Sander, and Brad J. Bushman. "Mirror, Mirror, on the Wall, Who's the Most Aggressive of Them All? Narcissism, Self-Esteem, and Aggression." In Shaver and Mikulincer. 203-19.

Thomas, Sandra P., ed. *Women and Anger.* Springer Publishing Co., 1993.

----------. "Anger and Its Manifestations in Women." In Thomas, *Women and Anger.* 40-67.

----------, and Madge M. Donnellan. "Stress, Role Responsibilities, Social Support, and Anger." In Thomas, *Women and Anger.* 112-28.

Thompson, Jerry. *My Life in the Klan.* G. P. Putnam's Sons, 1982.

Tiger, Lionel. *Men in Groups.* Random House, 1969.

Toch, Hans. *Violent Men: An Inquiry into the Psychology of Violence.* Aldine Publishing Co., 1969.

Todorov, Tzvetan. *Torture and the War on Terror.* Trans. Gila Walker. Seagull Books, 2009.

Travis, Jeremy. "Invisible Punishment: An Instrument of Social Exclusion." In Mauer and Chesney-Lind, 15-36.

Tsytsarev, Sergei V., and Gustavo R. Grodnitzky. "Anger and Criminality." In Kassinove, 91-108.

Turner, Carol. *Forgotten Heroes & Villains of Sand Creek.* The History Press, 2010.

Tuskegee Syphilis Study Ad Hoc Advisory Panel. "Interview with Four Survivors, Department of Health, Education and Welfare Study, 1973." In Reverby, *Tuskegee's Truths,* 132-35.

U.S. *No Gun Ri Review.* Office of the Inspector General, Department of the Army. January 2001.

Walter, Jess. *Ruby Ridge: The Truth & Tragedy of the Randy Weaver Family.* Regan Books, 2002.

[Watson], Martha Solomon. "The Rhetoric of Dehumanization: An Analysis of Medical Reports of the Tuskegee Syphilis Project." In Reverby, *Tuskegee's Truths,* 251-65.

Welsh-Huggins, Andrew. *Hatred at Home: Al-Qaida on Trial in the American Midwest.* Ohio Univ. Press, 2011.

Whitaker, Robert. *On the Laps of the Gods: The Red Summer of 1919 and the Struggle for Justice That Remade a Nation.* Crown Publishers, 2008.

Wolfe, Kathi. "The Disabled as a Target of Hate." In *Hate Crimes.* Ed. Jennifer Bussey. Greenhaven Press, 2007. 67-74.

Wolfgang, Marvin E., and Franco Ferracuti. *The Subculture of Violence: Towards an Integrated Theory of Criminology.* Tavistock Publications, 1967.

Woodruff, Paul. *The Ajax Dilemma: Justice, Fairness, and Rewards.* Oxford Univ.

Press, 2011.

Wormser, Richard. *Hoboes: Wandering in America, 1870-1940*. As quoted in Kinshasa, Kwando Mbiassi. *The Man from Scottsboro: Clarence Norris and the Infamous 1931 Alabama Rape Trial, in His Own Words*. McFarland & Co., 1997.

Wright, Stuart A., ed. *Armageddon in Waco: Critical Perspectives on the Branch Davidian Conflict*. Univ. of Chicago Press, 1995.

Young, Perry Deane. *God's Bullies: Native Reflections on Preachers and Politics*. Holt, Rinehart and Winston, 1982.

Zailckas, Koren. *Fury: A Memoir*. Viking, 2010.

Zillmann, Dolf. *Hostility and Aggression*. Lawrence Erlbaum Associates, 1979.

Zimring, Franklin E., and Gordon Hawkins. *Crime Is Not the Problem: Lethal Violence in America*. Oxford Univ. Press, 1997.

## About the Author

When H. L. Hix sees, as occasionally he does, a bumper sticker that reads, "Wyoming Is What America Was," he wonders what the person who affixed the bumper sticker construes it to mean, and what the person affirms of that meaning.

# Table of Contents

Aggression Cues ........................................................................... 1

    Aggression Cue 1: The presence of a gun. ......................... 2

    Aggression Cue 2: A hand slammed on a table. ............... 3

    Aggression Cue 3: A fist punched through sheetrock. ...... 4

    Aggression Cue 4: Arms crossed. ..................................... 5

    Aggression Cue 5: Fists clenched. .................................... 6

    Aggression Cue 6: A uniform. .......................................... 7

    Aggression Cue 7: The gathering of a crowd. ................. 8

    Aggression Cue 8: The presence of an aircraft carrier. .... 9

    Aggression Cue 9: Shouting. .......................................... 10

    Aggression Cue 10: Encroachment upon personal space. .. 11

    Aggression Cue 11: The stationing of troops. ................ 12

    Aggression Cue 12: Frequent interruption. .................... 13

    Aggression Cue 13: Use of expletives. ............................ 14

    Aggression Cue 14: Breaking of fragile items. ............... 15

    Aggression Cue 15: Obscene gestures. ........................... 16


The Plural of *Hate Speech* ....................................................... 19

    Preamble: Nomination Anthem ...................................... 20

    Days of 1852 .................................................................. 22

    Days of 1969 .................................................................. 22

    Compromised Sonnet: Compromising Report ............... 23

    Compromised Sonnet: Compromising Declaration ........ 23

    Compromised Sonnet: Compromising Inquest .............. 24

    Compromised Sonnet: Compromising Assembly ........... 24

    Compromised Sonnet: Compromising Analysis ............. 25

    Compromised Sonnet: Compromising Admonition ....... 25

    Compromised Sonnet: Compromising Discipline .......... 26

    Compromised Sonnet: Compromising Prophecy ........... 26

    Torture Ghazal ............................................................... 27

    Hate Crime Legislation Couplet ................................... 28

    "Get Tough" Sentencing and Prison Privatization Couplet .. 28

    Invisible Punishment Couplet ........................................ 28

Stealth Imperialism Couplet                                    29
God Hates Fags Couplet                                         29
What's the Big Deal About Torture Couplet                      29
Darwinian Rationale                                            30
Impellors and Inhibitors: Cultural, …                          30
Aryan Nations Couplets                                         31
What's Wrong With Kansas Stanzas                               31
Background Checks Quatrain                                     31
Futility Refrain                                               32
Bias-Crime Unit Sonnet                                         32
Thomas Jefferson Couplet                                       33
James Madison Couplet                                          33
George Washington Quatrains                                    33
God Is On Our Side Statistic                                   34
Cynical Political Solution Quatrain                            34
Let's Not Kid Ourselves Quatrain                               34
Militias / Malicious / Mollitious                              35
Compromised Sonnet: Compromising Imperative                    38
Compromised Sonnet: Compromising Prayer                        38
Compromised Sonnet: Compromising List                          39
Compromised Sonnet: Compromising Paean                         39
Compromised Sonnet: Compromising Interview                     40
Compromised Sonnet: Compromising Estimation                    40
Compromised Sonnet: Compromising Complaint                     41
Compromised Sonnet: Compromising Explanation                   41
Police Brutality Limerick                                      42
Survival Crimes Limerick                                       42
Short Anecdote in Which …                                      42
Compromised Sonnet: Compromising Association                   43
Compromised Sonnet: Compromising Search                        43
Compromised Sonnet: Compromising Definition                    44
Compromised Sonnet: Compromising Suppositions                  44
Compromised Sonnet: Compromising Contrast                      45
Compromised Sonnet: Compromising Debate                        45
Compromised Sonnet: Compromising Rationalization               46

Compromised Sonnet: Compromising Profile     46

American Ingenuity Villanelle     47

Foreign Policy Villanelle     47

Holding Cell Villanelle     48

Abortion Doctor Murder Villanelle     48

Paranoid Politics Villanelle     49

Sexual Violence Villanelle     49

Villanelle from the Case Files     50

Civilian Morale Villanelle     51

Crisis Orientation Villanelle     51

Arrest Warrant Villanelle     52

Ghetto Villanelle     52

Poverty Trap Villanelle     53

Psychopolitics Villanelle     53

Gun Culture Villanelle     54

Wartime Powers Villanelle     54

Addendum: Bill of Slights     55


The Anger Construct     59

Anger, considered by analogy with health and happiness:     60

Anger, considered as a state:     60

Anger, regardless of affect:     61

Anger contrasted to hatred:     61

Anger, not summative:     62

Anger, considered in relation to groups:     62

Anger, considered in light of the word's etymology:     63

Anger, as in former days they spoke of it:     63

Anger, by nomination:     64

Anger, by activation:     64

Anger, by protestation:     65

Anger, considered as a fundament:     65

Anger as rule rather than exception:     66

Anger, variously:     66

Anger, all in a row:     67

Anger, anger everywhere:     67

Anger, that willful naiveté:                                          68

Anger, considered as a right:                                        68

Anger, epidemic:                                                     69

Anger related to fear:                                               69

Anger as response:                                                   70

Anger as animus:                                                     70

Anger, synchronic and diachronic:                                    71

Anger less violent than pleasure:                                    71

Anger, erasing its tracks:                                           72

Anger theorized, v. 1:                                               72

Anger theorized, v. 2:                                               73

Anger theorized, v. 3:                                               73

Anger, easily mistaken:                                              74

Anger as misattributed and misplaced frustration:                   74

Anger, anaesthetic:                                                  75

Anger variables:                                                     75


Twenty Love Songs and a Measure of Disdain                           79

    Toxic Waste Love Song                                            80

    Criminal Tendencies Love Song                                    80

    Carcinogens Love Song                                            81

    Alternatives to Rage: Candidate One: Posturing                   81

    Corporate Greed and Irresponsibility Love Song                   82

    Your Lyin' Eyes Love Song                                        82

    Alternatives to Rage: Candidate Two:
        The Gisaro Ceremony                                          83

    Apocalyptic Endings Love Song                                    83

    Pathogens Love Song                                              84

    Invasive Species Love Song                                       84

    Alternatives to Rage: Candidate Three: Sa-Salan                  85

    Collision Course Love Song                                       85

    Mass Starvation Love Song                                        86

    Blood Sport Love Song                                            86

    Alternatives to Rage: Candidate Four: Quiet Biting Attack        87

    Numberless Casulaties Love Song                                  87

Devastating Journeys Love Song      88
Celebrity Murderers Love Song      88
Distance-Decay Function      88
Cyborg Love Song      89
Tables and Charts      89

Abscessive      93
I saved myself for *this?*      94
I worked hard and saved up for *this?*      95
I worked a second job all those years for *this?*      96
I quit smoking and drinking for *this?*      97
I risked my neck in those godforsaken jungles for *this?*      98
I risked my neck in that godforsaken desert for *this?*      99
I risked my neck in those godforsaken mountains for *this?*      100
I listened and took notes, for *this?*      101
I put myself through school for *this?*      102
All those committee meetings, for *this?*      103
I saved up all my sick days for *this?*      104
I stood in line all that time for *this?*      105
I worked out five days a week for *this?*      106
I paid the house note on time, month after month, for *this?*      107
I solicited all those donations for all those worthy causes, for *this?*      108
Every day I flossed, no exceptions, and for *this?*      109
I put three kids through school for *this?*      110
I changed all those diapers for *this?*      111
I cleaned up after him for twenty years for *this?*      112
I came back with half a leg for *this?*      113

God's Bounty      117
God's Bounty, as Stalking and Shooting from Cover      118
God's Bounty, as Normalization of the Pistol      118
God's Bounty, as Abundance and Ready Availability...      119
God's Bounty, as Unintended Consequences      120
God's Bounty, Qualified by Sundry Measures      120
God's Bounty, as Perpetual War      121
God's Bounty, as Data Sets on Firearms Use      122

God's Bounty, as a Secure Border                    123
God's Bounty, as the Image of Desire...             124


Erinyeneutics                                       133

Fire, Venom                                         134

Wounds, Recklessness                                135

Horse, Girl                                         136

Crop, Harvest                                       137

Shriek, Shiver                                      137

Fruit, Blood                                        138

As Best, Until                                      138

His Half, Your Half                                 139

Ever, When                                          139

Flood, Wave                                         140

Hers, Yours                                         140

Except, No Matter                                   141

Suspend, Rebut                                      141

Oaths, Inscription                                  142

Into, Against                                       143

Out Of, Away From                                   143

Into, Onto                                          144

Oracles, Dreams                                     144

Ships, Horses                                       145

Plea, Claim                                         145

Earthen, Olympian                                   146

True, Bent                                          147

And, And                                            147

Spirit, Dog                                         147

Banishment, Return                                  148

Demagogues, Sycophants                              149

Risk, Grief                                         149

Lashes, Luxury                                      150

Everything, Nothing                                 151

Fog, Hunger                                         152

Blood, Grapes                                       153

Figures, Phrases 153

Lost Wax 157
    Why *can't* anger occasion the calculated...? 158
    Must anger be expressed immediately? 161
    Does it have to look like anger to be anger? 161
    Are victims of the actions of the angry...? 162
    Have I *chosen* anger or been chosen by it? 164
    Who's entitled to host anger, and entitled by what? 164
    We learned our distance from the sun...? 165
    In what history is anger erased by...? 166
    What is it to be *overcome* with anger? 166

Apparatus 171
Attributions 172
Acknowledgments 174
Declaration 175
Disclaimer 176
Works Cited 177

# BOOKS FROM ETRUSCAN

*Zarathustra Must Die* | Dorian Alexander

*The Disappearance of Seth* | Kazim Ali

*Drift Ice* | Jennifer Atkinson

*Crow Man* | Tom Bailey

*Coronology* | Claire Bateman

*What We Ask of Flesh* | Remica L. Bingham

*The Greatest Jewish-American Lover in Hungarian History* | Michael Blumenthal

*No Hurry* | Michael Blumenthal

*Choir of the Wells* | Bruce Bond

*Cinder* | Bruce Bond

*The Other Sky* | Bruce Bond

*Peal* | Bruce Bond

*Poems and Their Making: A Conversation* | Moderated by Philip Brady

*Crave: Sojourn of a Hungry Soul* | Laurie Jean Cannady

*Toucans in the Arctic* | Scott Coffel

*Body of a Dancer* | Renée E. D'Aoust

*Scything Grace* | Sean Thomas Dougherty

*Surrendering Oz* | Bonnie Friedman

*Nahoonkara* | Peter Grandbois

*The Confessions of Doc Williams & Other Poems* | William Heyen

*The Football Corporations* | William Heyen

*A Poetics of Hiroshima* | William Heyen

*Shoah Train* | William Heyen

*September 11, 2001: American Writers Respond* | Edited by William Heyen

*As Easy As Lying* | H. L. Hix

*As Much As, If Not More Than* | H. L. Hix

*Chromatic* | H. L. Hix

*First Fire, Then Birds* | H. L. Hix

*God Bless* | H. L. Hix

*I'm Here to Learn to Dream in Your Language* | H. L. Hix

*Incident Light* | H. L. Hix

*Legible Heavens* | H. L. Hix

*Lines of Inquiry* | H. L. Hix

*Shadows of Houses* | H. L. Hix

*Wild and Whirling Words: A Poetic Conversation* | Moderated by H. L. Hix

*Art Into Life* | Frederick R. Karl

*Free Concert: New and Selected Poems* | Milton Kessler

*Parallel Lives* | Michael Lind

*The Burning House* | Paul Lisicky

*Quick Kills* | Lynn Lurie

*The Subtle Bodies* | James McCorkle

*Synergos* | Roberto Manzano

*The Gambler's Nephew* | Jack Matthews

*An Archaeology of Yearning* | Bruce Mills

*Arcadia Road* | Thorpe Moeckel

*Venison* | Thorpe Moeckel

*So Late, So Soon* | Carol Moldaw

*The Widening* | Carol Moldaw

*Cannot Stay* | Kevin Oderman

*White Vespa* | Kevin Oderman

*The Shyster's Daughter* | Paula Priamos

*Help Wanted: Female* | Sara Pritchard

*American Amnesiac* | Diane Raptosh

*Saint Joe's Passion* | JD Schraffenberger

*Lies Will Take You Somewhere* | Sheila Schwartz

*Fast Animal* | Tim Seibles

*American Fugue* | Alexis Stamatis

*The Casanova Chronicles* | Myrna Stone

*The White Horse: A Colombian Journey* | Diane Thiel

*The Arsonist's Song Has Nothing to Do With Fire* | Allison Titus

*The Fugitive Self* | John Wheatcroft

*YOU.* | Joseph P. Wood

ETRUSCAN PRESS IS PROUD OF SUPPORT RECEIVED FROM

Wilkes University

Youngstown State University

The Ohio Arts Council

The Stephen & Jeryl Oristaglio Foundation

The Nathalie & James Andrews Foundation

The National Endowment for the Arts

The Ruth H. Beecher Foundation

The Bates-Manzano Fund

The New Mexico Community Foundation

Drs. Barbara Brothers & Gratia Murphy Endowment

The Rayen Foundation

The Pella Foundation

Founded in 2001 with a generous grant from the Oristaglio Foundation, Etruscan Press is a nonprofit cooperative of poets and writers working to produce and promote books that nurture the dialogue among genres, achieve a distinctive voice, and reshape the literary and cultural histories of which we are a part.

**etruscan press**
www.etruscanpress.org

Etruscan Press books may be ordered from

Consortium Book Sales and Distribution

800.283.3572

www.cbsd.com

Small Press Distribution

800.869.7553

www.spdbooks.org

Etruscan Press is a 501(c)(3) nonprofit organization.

Contributions to Etruscan Press are tax deductible

as allowed under applicable law.

For more information, a prospectus,

or to order one of our titles,

contact us at books@etruscanpress.org.